LEGAL RESEARCH EXERCISES

Following The Bluebook:
A Uniform System of Citation

Tenth Edition

By

Nancy P. Johnson
Law Librarian and Professor of Law
Georgia State University
College of Law Library

Susan T. Phillips
Director of the Law Library and Professor of Law
Dee J. Kelly Law Library
Texas Wesleyan University
School of Law

THOMSON

WEST

Mat #40760166

© West, a Thomson business, 2003, 2005
© 2008 Thomson/West
      610 Opperman Drive
      St. Paul, MN 55123
      1–800–313–9378

Printed in the United States of America

ISBN: 978–0–314–19536–4

 TEXT IS PRINTED ON 10% POST CONSUMER RECYCLED PAPER

TABLE OF CONTENTS

Student's Introduction

Assignment:

STUDENT'S INTRODUCTION

Mastering efficient research skills is more important than ever in the current legal environment. This tenth edition of *Legal Research Exercises, Following The Bluebook: A Uniform System of Citation* will help you learn to master efficient legal research skills. In completing the assignments in this book, you should become familiar with many kinds of research materials and you can use this familiarity to formulate basic research strategy. You will develop skills in using your law library and you will feel more comfortable with legal citation format.

We intend that none of the questions in this book to be extremely time consuming. If you cannot find an answer, ask your professor for help. Read the relevant material in your legal research text before attempting to complete the assignments. When we ask for a full citation, we want you to include the case name, reporter citation, court (if necessary) and a year in your citation, as specified by *The Bluebook: A Uniform System of Citation* (18th ed.).

With two exceptions, the assignments contain four variations (A, B, C, D). Exercises A and B are written to be completed using paper resources. Exercise C is written do be completed using Westlaw, and Exercise D should be completed using LexisNexis. The exceptions are Assignment Six, which has only three variations since its subject matter is the *American Law Reports* (A.L.R.). Since the A.L.R. annotations are not available on LexisNexis, there is not an Exercise D for this assignment. In addition, Assignment Ten has only two variations. Its Exercise A should be completed using the Internet, and its Exercise B should be completed using Westlaw and LexisNexis.

Practice professionalism by reshelving your books once you answer questions. It takes only a few seconds to reshelve the materials.

To supplement your in-class instruction and the materials in this legal research exercise book, you may want to review the CALI lessons on legal writing and legal research. You can find these lessons at http://www.cali.org.

We have tried very hard to eliminate all errors, but we apologize for any that you may discover. We have learned that no matter how painstaking our efforts are in this regard, because of the republishing of legal materials, errors creep into a book of this nature as time passes. Please contact your professors when you discover a problem.

Nancy P. Johnson
Georgia State University
College of Law
njohnson@gsu.edu

Susan T. Phillips
Dee J. Kelly Law Library
Texas Wesleyan University School of Law
sphillips@law.txwes.edu

GOALS OF THIS ASSIGNMENT:
To teach you how to find cases when you have citations.
To acquaint you with the location of reporters in your law library.
To familiarize you with the rules for citing cases in *The Bluebook: A Uniform System of Citation*, 18th ed.

CITATION RULES: Read the *Introduction*, Bluepages B1, Bluepages B5.1- B5.1.3, Rules 6.1, 10.2.1, 10.2.2, 10.3.1, 10.3.2, 10.4, 10.5, 18, 18.1, 18.1.1 and refer to tables BT.2, T.1, T.6, and T.10 of *The Bluebook*. Apply these rules as you learn the correct citation for each case.

Throughout this book, when we ask that you provide a full citation, give the name, citation and date of the case, and any other necessary information (such as court) required by *The Bluebook*.

The first two questions introduce you to the rules for citing U.S. Supreme Court cases. **Example: *Loving v. Virginia*, 388 U.S. 1 (1967).**

United States Reports, abbreviated U.S. in case citation, is the official reporter. Note that no parallel, unofficial reporters are listed for U.S. Supreme Court cases when a U.S. citation is available. At the beginning of table T.1 in *The Bluebook*, read the instructions for the **Supreme Court**.

1. If an opinion of the U.S. Supreme Court has not yet been published in *United States Reports*, which unofficial reporters should you cite instead, in order of preference?

2. State the full citation for 540 U.S. 419.

The third question requires you to find and cite a U.S. Supreme Court case from before 1875. They published these cases in reporters known as **nominative** reporters, because they were generally known by the name of the person who compiled the volume. The form of citation for a case in a nominative reporter differs from the form for a case appearing in contemporary sources. Study the rules for citing cases found in nominative reporters (*The Bluebook* calls them "early American reporters." See Rule 10.3.2.). Here is an example of how to cite a U.S. Supreme Court nominative reporter: *Hughes v. Union Ins. Co.*, **21 U.S. (8 Wheat.) 294 (1823).**

3.   State the full citation for 33 U.S. 88. Note: For the date, use the year of the Court Term.

Next, you must find and cite a federal court of appeals case from a circuit. When citing a court of appeals case, always list the circuit within the parentheses, along with the date. **Example:** *Bonilla v. Volvo Car Corp.*, **150 F.3d 62 (1st Cir. 1998).**

4.   State the full citation for 498 F.3d 634.

Now, find and cite a federal district court case. When citing a case from district court, the particular court is included within the parentheses. **Example:** *Hillard v. Guidant Corp.*, **76 F. Supp. 2d 566 (M.D. Pa. 1999).**

5.   State the full citation for 505 F. Supp. 2d 704. Note: The district is listed before the state--the division, if listed, is listed after. Always include the district in the citation, never the division.

In general, for state decisions the state and the name of the court should be included within the parentheses. However, do not include the name of the court if the court of decision is the highest court of the state. Here is an example of how to cite a Pennsylvania Supreme Court case. How do you know what to include in the parentheses? Read Rule 10.4(b) and look at the listing for Pennsylvania in table T.1. **Example: *Commonwealth v. Brayboy*, 246 A.2d 675 (Pa. 1968).**

Find 920 A.2d 73 to answer Questions 6 and 7.

6.   State the full citation for 920 A.2d 73.

Should you ever cite the official version of a case? Yes, if the case is very old and there is no regional citation. Otherwise, you should cite it **only** if you are **including it in a document submitted to a state court whose local rules require citation to the official reporter.** (See Rule 10.3.1(a), Bluepages B5.1.3, and table BT.2.) Here is our previous example cited in such a context. **Example: *Commonwealth v. Brayboy,* 431 Pa. 365, 246 A.2d 675 (1968). Note**: We followed Rule 10.4(b) and omitted the jurisdiction Pa. from the parentheses because it is unambiguously conveyed by the reporter title.

7.   State the full citation for 920 A.2d 73, assuming you are including this citation in a document submitted to a Connecticut state court whose local rules require citing to the official report volume.

Next, find an opinion from a state intermediate appellate court and cite it correctly. **Example: *Maluszewski v. Allstate Ins. Co.*, 640 A.2d 129 (Conn. App. Ct. 1994).**

Find 233 S.W.3d 689 to answer Questions 8 and 9.

8.   State the full citation for 233 S.W.3d 689.

Our previous example of an intermediate state appellate court citation cited in a document submitted to a Connecticut state court whose local rules require citing to the official report volume would look like this. **Example:** *Maluszewski v. Allstate Ins. Co.*, **34 Conn. App. 27, 640 A.2d 129 (1994).**

9.   State the full citation for 233 S.W.3d 689, assuming you are including this citation in a document to an Arkansas state court whose local rules require citing to the official report volume.

You should be aware that not all appellate court decisions are designated to be published by the issuing court.   These cases are called **"unpublished"** or **"unreported"** cases.   Historically, an attorney was not permitted to cite to an unpublished case except in very limited circumstances.   However in recent years, some jurisdictions have amended their court rules to allow citing unpublished cases. For example, the Federal Rules of Appellate Procedure provide that a court must allow the citation of any unpublished federal opinion issued on or after Jan. 1, 2007 (FRAP 32.1). Check your federal circuit's local court rules to determine if opinions issued before Jan. 1, 2007 may be cited. In addition, you should check your state's court rules and determine whether or not you are permitted to cite to unreported state cases in state court.

Typically, unpublished cases can be found on the court's own Internet page as well as on Westlaw and LexisNexis.

Sign on to Westlaw at <u>http://lawschool.westlaw.com</u>.

10. Select the **CTAU** database which contains the Court of Appeals' unreported opinions. You can access this database by one of two ways: 1) start in the main directory and link to the following sequence **U.S. Federal Materials > Federal Cases & Judicial Materials > U.S. Court of Appeals Cases, Unreported**; or 2) type "**CTAU**" in the **"Search for a database"** box. Search for the 2008 United States Court of Appeals, Fifth Circuit case with docket number 07-30524. Provide the proper citation according to Rule 18.1.1.

GOALS OF THIS ASSIGNMENT:
To teach you how to find cases when you have citations.
To acquaint you with the location of reporters in your law library.
To familiarize you with the rules for citing cases in *The Bluebook: A Uniform System of Citation*, 18th ed.

CITATION RULES: Read the *Introduction*, Bluepages B1, Bluepages B5.1- B5.1.3, Rules 6.1, 10.2.1, 10.2.2, 10.3.1, 10.3.2, 10.4, 10.5, 18, 18.1, 18.1.1 and refer to tables BT.2, T.1, T.6, and T.10 of *The Bluebook*. Apply these rules as you learn the correct citation for each case.

Throughout this book, when we ask that you provide a full citation, give the name, citation and date of the case, and any other necessary information (such as court) required by *The Bluebook*.

The first two questions introduce you to the rules for citing U.S. Supreme Court cases. **Example: *Loving v. Virginia,* 388 U.S. 1 (1967).**

United States Reports, abbreviated U.S. in case citation, is the official reporter. Note that no parallel, unofficial reporters are listed for U.S. Supreme Court cases when a U.S. citation is available. At the beginning of table T.1 in *The Bluebook*, read the instructions for the **Supreme Court**.

1.   If an opinion of the U.S. Supreme Court has not yet been published in *United States Reports*, which unofficial reporters should you cite instead, in order of preference?

2.   State the full citation for 541 U.S. 509.

The third question requires you to find and cite a U.S. Supreme Court case from before 1875. They published these cases in reporters known as **nominative** reporters, because they were generally known by the name of the person who compiled the volume. The form of citation for a case in a nominative reporter differs from the form for a case appearing in contemporary sources. Study the rules for citing cases found in nominative reporters (*The Bluebook* calls them "early American reporters." See Rule 10.3.2.). Here is an example of how to cite a U.S. Supreme Court nominative reporter: ***Hughes v. Union Ins. Co.*, 21 U.S. (8 Wheat.) 294 (1823).**

3.   State the full citation for 81 U.S. 472. **Note**: For the date, use the year of the Court Term.

Next, you must find and cite a federal court of appeals case from a circuit. When citing a court of appeals case, always list the circuit within the parentheses, along with the date. **Example: *Bonilla v. Volvo Car Corp.*, 150 F.3d 62 (1st Cir. 1998).**

4.   State the full citation for 501 F.3d 630.

Now, find and cite a federal district court case. When citing a case from district court, the particular court is included within the parentheses. **Example: *Hillard v. Guidant Corp.*, 76 F. Supp. 2d 566 (M.D. Pa. 1999).**

5.   State the full citation for 513 F. Supp. 2d 96. Note: The district is listed before the state—the division, if listed, is listed after. Always include the district in the citation, never the division.

In general, for state decisions the state and the name of the court should be included within the parentheses. However, do not include the name of the court if the court of decision is the highest court of the state. Here is an example of how to cite a Pennsylvania Supreme Court case. How do you know what to include in the parentheses? Read Rule 10.4(b) and look at the listing for Pennsylvania in table T.1. **Example:** *Commonwealth v. Brayboy*, **246 A.2d 675 (Pa. 1968).**

Find 607 S.E.2d 803 to answer Questions 6 and 7.

6. State the full citation for 607 S.E.2d 803.

Should you ever cite the official version of a case? Yes, if the case is very old and there is no regional citation. Otherwise, you should cite it **only** if you are **including it in a document submitted to a state court whose local rules require citation to the official reporter.** (See Rule 10.3.1(a), Bluepages B5.1.3, and table BT.2.) Here is our previous example cited in such a context. **Example:** *Commonwealth v. Brayboy,* **431 Pa. 365, 246 A.2d 675 (1968). Note**: We followed Rule 10.4(b) and omitted the jurisdiction Pa. from the parentheses because it is unambiguously conveyed by the reporter title.

7. State the full citation for 607 S.E.2d 803, assuming you are including this citation in a document submitted to a West Virginia state court whose local rules require citing to the official report volume.

Next, find an opinion from a state intermediate appellate court and cite it correctly. **Example:** *Maluszewski v. Allstate Ins. Co.*, **640 A.2d 129 (Conn. App. Ct. 1994).**

Find 706 N.W.2d 569 to answer Questions 8 and 9.

8.   State the full citation for 706 N.W.2d 569.

Our previous example of an intermediate state appellate court citation cited in a document submitted to a Connecticut state court whose local rules require citing to the official report volume would look like this. **Example:** *Maluszewski v. Allstate Ins. Co.*, **34 Conn. App. 27, 640 A.2d 129 (1994).**

9.   State the full citation for 706 N.W.2d 569, assuming you are including this citation in a document to a Nebraska state court whose local rules require citing to the official report volume.

You should be aware that not all appellate court decisions are designated to be published by the issuing court.   These cases are called **"unpublished"** or **"unreported"** cases.   Historically, an attorney was not permitted to cite to an unpublished case except in very limited circumstances.   However in recent years, some jurisdictions have amended their court rules to allow citing unpublished cases.   For example, the Federal Rules of Appellate Procedure provide that a court must allow the citation of any unpublished federal opinion issued on or after Jan. 1, 2007 (FRAP 32.1).   Check your federal circuit's local court rules to determine if opinions issued before Jan. 1, 2007 may be cited.   In addition, you should check your state's court rules and determine whether or not you are permitted to cite to unreported state cases in state court.

Typically, unpublished cases can be found on the court's own Internet page as well as on Westlaw and LexisNexis.

Sign on to Westlaw at <u>http://lawschool.westlaw.com</u>.

10. Select the **CTAU** database which contains the Court of Appeals' unreported opinions. You can access this database by one of two ways: 1) start in the main directory and link to the following sequence **U.S. Federal Materials > Federal Cases & Judicial Materials > U.S. Court of Appeals Cases, Unreported**; or 2) type "**CTAU**" in the "**Search for a database**" box. Search for the 2008 United States Court of Appeals, Eleventh Circuit case with docket number 06-00272-CV-ODE-1. Provide the proper citation according to Rule 18.1.1.

ASSIGNMENT ONE
FINDING AND CITING CASES
EXERCISE C

GOALS OF THIS ASSIGNMENT:
To teach you how to find cases on Westlaw when you have citations.
To familiarize you with the rules for citing cases in *The Bluebook: A Uniform System of Citation*, 18th ed.

CITATION RULES: Read the *Introduction*, Bluepages B1, Bluepages B5.1- B5.1.3, Rules 6.1, 10.2.1, 10.2.2, 10.3.1, 10.3.2, 10.4, 10.5, 18, 18.1, 18.1.1 and refer to tables BT.2, T.1, T.6, and T.10 of *The Bluebook*. Since Rule 18 requires citation of traditional printed sources, cite these reported cases to their printed sources. Apply these rules as you learn the correct citation for each case.

Throughout this book, when we ask that you provide a full citation, give the name, citation and date of the case, and any other necessary information (such as court) required by *The Bluebook*.

The first two questions introduce you to the rules for citing U.S. Supreme Court cases. **Example: *Loving v. Virginia*, 388 U.S. 1 (1967).**

United States Reports, abbreviated U.S. in case citation, is the official reporter. Note that no parallel, unofficial reporters are listed for U.S. Supreme Court cases when a U.S. citation is available. At the beginning of table T.1 in *The Bluebook*, read the instructions for the **Supreme Court**.

1.   If an opinion of the U.S. Supreme Court has not yet been published in *United States Reports*, which unofficial reporters should you cite instead, in order of preference?

Sign on to Westlaw at http://lawschool.westlaw.com.

2.   Use **Find** to retrieve 542 U.S. 600. State the full citation for 542 U.S. 600.

The third question requires you to find and cite a U.S. Supreme Court case from before 1875. They published these cases in reporters known as **nominative** reporters, because they were generally known by the name of the person who compiled the volume. The form of citation for a case in a nominative reporter differs from the form for a case appearing in contemporary sources. Study the rules for citing cases found in nominative reporters (*The Bluebook* calls them "early American reporters." See Rule 10.3.2.). Here is an example of how to cite a U.S. Supreme Court nominative reporter: *Hughes v. Union Ins. Co.*, **21 U.S. (8 Wheat.) 294 (1823).**

3.   Use **Find** to retrieve 55 U.S. 505. State the full citation for 55 U.S. 505. **Note**: For the date, use the year of the Court Term.

Next, you must find and cite a federal court of appeals case from a circuit. When citing a court of appeals case, always list the circuit within the parentheses, along with the date. **Example:** *Bonilla v. Volvo Car Corp.*, **150 F.3d 62 (1st Cir. 1998).**

4.   Use **Find** to retrieve 505 F.3d 785. State the full citation for 505 F.3d 785.

Now, find and cite a federal district court case. When citing a case from district court, the particular court is included within the parentheses. **Example:** *Hillard v. Guidant Corp.*, **76 F. Supp. 2d 566 (M.D. Pa. 1999).**

5.   Use **Find** to retrieve 518 F. Supp. 2d 977. State the full citation for 518 F. Supp. 2d 977. **Note:** The district is listed before the state—the division, if listed, is listed after. Always include the district in the citation, never the division.

In general, for state decisions the state and the name of the court should be included within the parentheses. However, do not include the name of the court if the court of decision is the highest court of the state. Here is an example of how to cite a Pennsylvania Supreme Court case. How do you know what to include in the parentheses? Read Rule 10.4(b) and look at the listing for Pennsylvania in table T.1. **Example:** *Commonwealth v. Brayboy*, **246 A.2d 675 (Pa. 1968).**

Use Find to retrieve 170 P.3d 1049 to answer Questions 6 and 7.

6.   State the full citation for 170 P.3d 1049.

Should you ever cite the official version of a case? Yes, if the case is very old and there is no regional citation. Otherwise, you should cite it **only** if you are **including it in a document submitted to a state court whose local rules require citation to the official reporter.** (See Rule 10.3.1(a), Bluepages B5.1.3, and table BT.2.) Here is our previous example cited in such a context. **Example:** *Commonwealth v. Brayboy,* **431 Pa. 365, 246 A.2d 675 (1968).** Note: We followed Rule 10.4(b) and omitted the jurisdiction Pa. from the parentheses because it is unambiguously conveyed by the reporter title.

7.   State the full citation for 170 P.3d 1049, assuming you are including this citation in a document submitted to an Oregon state court whose local rules require citing to the official report volume.

Next, find an opinion from a state intermediate appellate court and cite it correctly. **Example:** *Maluszewski v. Allstate Ins. Co.*, **640 A.2d 129 (Conn. App. Ct. 1994).**

Use Find to retrieve 856 N.E.2d 900 to answer Questions 8 and 9.

8.   State the full citation for 856 N.E.2d 900.

Our previous example of an intermediate state appellate court citation cited in a document submitted to a Connecticut state court whose local rules require citing to the official report volume would look like this. **Example:** *Maluszewski v. Allstate Ins. Co.*, **34 Conn. App. 27, 640 A.2d 129 (1994).**

9.   State the full citation for 856 N.E.2d 900, assuming you are including this citation in a document to a Massachusetts state court whose local rules require citing to the official report volume.

You should be aware that not all appellate court decisions are designated to be published by the issuing court. These cases are called **"unpublished"** or **"unreported"** cases. Historically, an attorney was not permitted to cite to an unpublished case except in very limited circumstances. However in recent years, some jurisdictions have amended their court rules to allow citing unpublished cases. For example, the Federal Rules of Appellate Procedure provide that a court must allow the citation of any unpublished federal opinion issued on or after Jan. 1, 2007 (FRAP 32.1). Check your federal circuit's local court rules to determine if opinions issued before Jan. 1, 2007 may be cited. In addition, you should check your state's court rules and determine whether or not you are permitted to cite to unreported state cases in state court.

Typically, unpublished cases can be found on the court's own Internet page as well as on Westlaw and LexisNexis.

10.   Select the **CTAU** database which contains the Court of Appeals' unreported opinions. You can access this database by one of two ways: 1) start in the main directory and link to the following sequence **U.S. Federal Materials > Federal Cases & Judicial Materials > U.S. Court of Appeals Cases, Unreported**; or 2) type "**CTAU**" in the **"Search for a database"** box. Search for the 2008 United States Court of Appeals, Tenth Circuit case with docket number 07-9523. Provide the proper citation according to Rule 18.1.1.

ASSIGNMENT ONE
FINDING AND CITING CASES
EXERCISE D

GOALS OF THIS ASSIGNMENT:
To teach you how to find cases on LexisNexis when you have citations.
To familiarize you with the rules for citing cases in *The Bluebook: A Uniform System of Citation*, 18th ed.

CITATION RULES: Read the *Introduction*, Bluepages B1, Bluepages B5.1- B5.1.3, Rules 6.1, 10.2.1, 10.2.2, 10.3.1, 10.3.2, 10.4, 10.5, 18, 18.1, 18.1.1 and refer to tables BT.2, T.1, T.6, and T.10 of *The Bluebook*.   Since Rule 18 requires citation of traditional printed sources, cite these reported cases to their printed sources. Apply these rules as you learn the correct citation for each case.

Throughout this book, when we ask that you provide a full citation, give the name, citation and date of the case, and any other necessary information (such as court) required by *The Bluebook*.

The first two questions introduce you to the rules for citing U.S. Supreme Court cases. **Example: *Loving v. Virginia*, 388 U.S. 1 (1967).**

United States Reports, abbreviated U.S. in case citation, is the official reporter. Note that no parallel, unofficial reporters are listed for U.S. Supreme Court cases when a U.S. citation is available. At the beginning of table T.1 in *The Bluebook*, read the instructions for the **Supreme Court**.

1.   If an opinion of the U.S. Supreme Court has not yet been published in *United States Reports*, which unofficial reporters should you cite instead, in order of preference?

        Sign on to LexisNexis at <u>http://www.lexisnexis.com/lawschool</u>.

2.   Use **Get a Document** to retrieve 543 U.S. 405. State the full citation for 543 U.S. 405.

The third question requires you to find and cite a U.S. Supreme Court case from before 1875. They published these cases in reporters known as **nominative** reporters, because they were generally known by the name of the person who compiled the volume. The form of citation for a case in a nominative reporter differs from the form for a case appearing in contemporary sources. Study the rules for citing cases found in nominative reporters (*The Bluebook* calls them "early American reporters." See Rule 10.3.2.). Here is an example of how to cite a U.S. Supreme Court nominative reporter: ***Hughes v. Union Ins. Co.*, 21 U.S. (8 Wheat.) 294 (1823).**

3.   Use **Get a Document** to retrieve 67 U.S. 481. State the full citation for 67 U.S. 481. **Note**: For the date, use the year of the Court Term.

Next, you must find and cite a federal court of appeals case from a circuit. When citing a court of appeals case, always list the circuit within the parentheses, along with the date. **Example: *Bonilla v. Volvo Car Corp.*, 150 F.3d 62 (1st Cir. 1998).**

4.   Use **Get a Document** to retrieve 510 F.3d 550. State the full citation for 510 F.3d 550.

Now, find and cite a federal district court case. When citing a case from district court, the particular court is included within the parentheses. **Example: *Hillard v. Guidant Corp.*, 76 F. Supp. 2d 566 (M.D. Pa. 1999).**

5.   Use **Get a Document** to retrieve 522 F. Supp. 2d 452. State the full citation for 522 F. Supp. 2d 452. **Note**: The district is listed before the state—the division, if listed, is listed after. Always include the district in the citation, never the division.

In general, for state decisions the state and the name of the court should be included within the parentheses. However, do not include the name of the court if the court of decision is the highest court of the state. Here is an example of how to cite a Pennsylvania Supreme Court case. How do you know what to include in the parentheses? Read Rule 10.4(b) and look at the listing for Pennsylvania in table T.1. **Example:** ***Commonwealth v. Brayboy*, 246 A.2d 675 (Pa. 1968).**

Use Get a Document to retrieve 140 P.3d 377 to answer Questions 6 and 7.

6.   State the full citation for 140 P.3d 377.

Should you ever cite the official version of a case? Yes, if the case is very old and there is no regional citation. Otherwise, you should cite it **only** if you are **including it in a document submitted to a state court whose local rules require citation to the official reporter.** (See Rule 10.3.1(a), Bluepages B5.1.3, and table BT.2.) Here is our previous example cited in such a context. **Example:** ***Commonwealth v. Brayboy*, 431 Pa. 365, 246 A.2d 675 (1968).** Note: We followed Rule 10.4(b) and omitted the jurisdiction Pa. from the parentheses because it is unambiguously conveyed by the reporter title.

7.   State the full citation for 140 P.3d 377, assuming you are including this citation in a document submitted to a Hawaii state court whose local rules require citing to the official report volume.

Next, find an opinion from a state intermediate appellate court and cite it correctly. **Example:** ***Maluszewski v. Allstate Ins. Co.*, 640 A.2d 129 (Conn. App. Ct. 1994).**

Use Get a Document to retrieve 936 A.2d 388 to answer Questions 8 and 9.

8.   State the full citation for 936 A.2d 388.

Our previous example of an intermediate state appellate court citation cited in a document submitted to a Connecticut state court whose local rules require citing to the official report volume would look like this. **Example:** *Maluszewski v. Allstate Ins. Co.*, **34 Conn. App. 27, 640 A.2d 129 (1994).**

9.   State the full citation for 936 A.2d 388, assuming you are including this citation in a document to a Maryland state court whose local rules require citing to the official report volume.

You should be aware that not all appellate court decisions are designated to be published by the issuing court. These cases are called **"unpublished"** or **"unreported"** cases. Historically, an attorney was not permitted to cite to an unpublished case except in very limited circumstances. However in recent years, some jurisdictions have amended their court rules to allow citing unpublished cases. For example, the Federal Rules of Appellate Procedure provide that a court must allow the citation of any unpublished federal opinion issued on or after Jan. 1, 2007 (FRAP 32.1). Check your federal circuit's local court rules to determine if opinions issued before Jan. 1, 2007 may be cited. In addition, you should check your state's court rules and determine whether or not you are permitted to cite to unreported state cases in state court.

Typically, unpublished cases can be found on the court's own Internet page as well as on Westlaw and LexisNexis.

10.   Select the following source which contains the United States Court of Appeals, Ninth Circuit reported and unreported opinions: **Legal > Cases – U.S. > U.S. Courts of Appeals – By Circuit > 9th Circuit – US Court of Appeals Cases & Bankruptcy Appellate Panel**. Search for the 2008 United States Court of Appeals, Fifth Circuit case with docket number 07-30524. Provide the proper citation according to Rule 18.1.1.

ASSIGNMENT TWO
SUPREME COURT REPORTERS AND PARTS OF A CASE
EXERCISE A

GOALS OF THIS ASSIGNMENT:
To familiarize you with the parts of a case in three different reporters.
To introduce you to star paging.

CITATION RULES: Use *The Bluebook: A Uniform System of Citation*, 18th ed., Rules 10.2, 10.2.1, 10.2.2, 10.3.1, 10.3.2, 10.4, 10.5, and tables T.1, T.6, and T.10. Use the format for court documents and legal memoranda and assume that the case citation appears in a citation sentence.

Locate 416 U.S. 115 to answer Questions 1-9.

1.   Find 416 U.S. 115. This is the official reporter version of the case. What is the case name? Use correct form (Rule 10.2).

2.   On what date was the case decided?

3.   What is the docket number of the case?

4.   Which party is the respondent?

5.   Which Justice wrote the opinion of the Court?

6.   Which Justice wrote the dissenting opinion?

7. What was the lower court cite of this case, on its way up to the Supreme Court? **Note**: You are looking for the cite of an F.2d case.

8. How did the Supreme Court act on the judgment of the court below?

9. Who argued the cause for the petitioner?

To answer Questions 10-17 you will need to compare the case from Question 1 in the two unofficial versions, S. Ct., L. Ed., of this opinion.

10. Find the appropriate book of vol. 94 of the *Supreme Court Reporter* (S. Ct.), published by West, and vol. 40 of the *U.S. Supreme Court Reports--Lawyers' Edition* (L. Ed. 2d), published then by Lawyers Co-operative Publishing Company and now by LexisNexis. These two reporters are unofficial reporters for United States Supreme Court cases. Use the Cases Reported table at the front of S. Ct. and the Table of Cases Reported in the front of L. Ed. to find your case in both reporters.

  a. What is the S. Ct. cite?

  b. What is the L. Ed. 2d cite?

11. Examine the headnotes preceding the opinions. On which page of which reporter does the second West topic and key number appear? **Note**: A small key-shaped symbol accompanies the West topic and key number.

12.   State the West topic and key number from the preceding question.

13.   Each headnote corresponds to a particular part of the Court's opinion. Examine the opinion in S. Ct. and look for references to the headnote numbers (boldface numbers in brackets **[1]**). On which page of the S. Ct. **opinion** is there a reference to the second West headnote?

14.   Star paging enables attorneys using L. Ed. or S. Ct. to cite U.S. paging without having U.S. itself. Star paging in L. Ed. is shown thus: **[405 US 729]**. Star paging in S. Ct. is indicated thus: ⊥**729**. Looking at the *Supreme Court Reporter* and using star paging ⊥, state the page of *United States Reports* (U.S.) on which the corresponding material related to the second **[2]** West headnote begins.

15.   Notice that the two unofficial reporters have different headnotes. How many headnotes are in the *U.S. Supreme Court Reports, Lawyers' Edition*?

16.   Question 8 asked you about the **disposition** of the case, that is, how the Supreme Court treated the judgment of the court below. The **holding** is another part of a case, the application of rules of law to the specific key facts in the case. Did the court hold that a party may still have sufficient interests and injury to justify declaratory relief even though the underlying case for an injunction ended with the settlement of the strike? You may want to review the syllabus of the case.

17.   Blackmun's opinion states that the facts of this case provide full and complete satisfaction of the requirement that a case or controversy exists between the parties. What two laws are cited as to this requirement?

GOALS OF THIS ASSIGNMENT:
To familiarize you with the parts of a case in three different reporters.
To introduce you to star paging.

CITATION RULES: Use *The Bluebook: A Uniform System of Citation*, 18th ed., Rules 10.2, 10.2.1, 10.2.2, 10.3.1, 10.3.2, 10.4, 10.5, and tables T.1, T.6, and T.10. Use the format for court documents and legal memoranda and assume that the case citation appears in a citation sentence.

Locate 426 U.S. 794 to answer Questions 1-9.

1.　　Find 426 U.S. 794. This is the official reporter version of the case. What is the case name? Use correct form (Rule 10.2).

2.　　On what date was the case decided?

3.　　What is the docket number of the case?

4.　　Which party is the appellee?

5.　　Which Justice wrote the opinion of the Court?

6.　　Which Justice wrote a dissenting opinion?

7.   What was the lower court cite of this case, on its way up to the Supreme Court? **Note**: You are looking for the cite of an F. Supp. case.

8.   How did the Supreme Court act on the judgment of the court below?

9.   Who argued the cause for the appellee?

To answer Questions 10-17, you will need to compare the case from Question 1 in the two unofficial versions, S. Ct., L. Ed., of this opinion.

10.   Find the appropriate book of vol. 96 of the *Supreme Court Reporter* (S. Ct.), published by West, and vol. 49 of the *U.S. Supreme Court Reports—Lawyers' Edition* (L. Ed. 2d), published then by Lawyers Co-operative Publishing Company and now by LexisNexis. These two reporters are unofficial reporters for United States Supreme Court cases. Use the Cases Reported table at the front of S. Ct. and the Table of Cases Reported in the front of L. Ed. to find your case in both reporters.

   a.   What is the S. Ct. cite?

   b.   What is the L. Ed. 2d cite?

11.   Examine the headnotes preceding the opinions. On what page of which reporter does the fourth West topic and key number appear? **Note**: A small key-shaped symbol accompanies the West topic and key number.

12.   State the West topic and key number from the preceding question.

13.   Each headnote corresponds to a particular part of the Court's opinion. Examine the opinion in S. Ct. and look for references to the headnote numbers (boldface numbers in brackets **[1]**). On what page of the S. Ct. **opinion** is there a reference to the fourth West headnote?

14.   Star paging enables attorneys using L. Ed. or S. Ct. to cite U.S. paging without using U.S. itself. Star paging in L. Ed. is shown thus: **[405 US 729]**. Star paging in S. Ct. is indicated thus: ⊥**729.** Looking at the *Supreme Court Reporter* and using star paging ⊥, state the page of *United States Reports* (U.S.) on which the corresponding material related to the fourth **[4]** West headnote begins.

15.   Notice that the two unofficial reporters have different headnotes. How many headnotes are in the *U.S. Supreme Court Reports, Lawyers' Edition*?

16.   Question 8 asked you about the **disposition** of the case, that is, how the Supreme Court treated the judgment of the court below. The **holding** is another part of a case, the application of rules of law to the specific key facts in the case. Did the court hold that the statutory scheme for paying bounties to Maryland scrap processors did not constitute an impermissible burden on interstate commerce?

17.   The Court in this case also looked at whether or not the Maryland statutory scheme passed equal protection scrutiny. Where do you find the Equal Protection Clause?

ASSIGNMENT TWO
SUPREME COURT REPORTERS AND PARTS OF A CASE
EXERCISE C

GOALS OF THIS ASSIGNMENT:
To familiarize you with the parts of a case on Westlaw.
To introduce you to star paging.

CITATION RULES: Use *The Bluebook: A Uniform System of Citation*, 18th ed., Rules 10.2, 10.2.1, 10.2.2, 10.3.1, 10.3.2, 10.4, 10.5, 18, and tables T.1, T.6, and T.10. Use the format for court documents and legal memoranda and assume that the case citation appears in a citation sentence.

Sign onto Westlaw at http://lawschool.westlaw.com and use Find to retrieve 544 U.S. 167.

1.   What is the case name? Use correct form (Rule 10.2).

2.   On what date was the case decided?

3.   What is the docket number of the case?

4.   Which party is the respondent?

5.   Which Justice wrote the opinion of the Court?

6.   Which Justice wrote a dissenting opinion?

7. What was the lower court cite of this case, on its way up to the Supreme Court? **Note**: You are looking for the cite of an F.3d case.

8. How did the Supreme Court act on the judgment of the court below?

9. Who argued the cause for the respondent?

10. You found this case on Westlaw using its official *United States Reports* cite. Notice that Westlaw provides you with the citations to several other unofficial versions including the *Supreme Court Reporter* (S. Ct.), published by West, and the *U.S. Supreme Court Reports—Lawyers' Edition* (L. Ed. 2d), published by LexisNexis. These two reporters are unofficial reporters for United States Supreme Court cases.

   a. What is the S. Ct. cite?

   b. What is the L. Ed. 2d cite?

11. The West editors add headnotes to the beginning of each case. The editors write a headnote, or summary, for each point of law in the case. Examine the headnotes preceding the opinion. How many headnotes have the West editors written for this case?

12. The West editors assign at least one West topic and key number to each headnote. On Westlaw, you see the full analysis for the topic and key number. You see the topic, its assigned topic number, then there is a "k" standing for key number, with the last portion of the number being the key number that appears in the digest. Therefore, you must look at the last line of the topic/key number analysis for the topic and key number assigned to the headnote. State the West topic name and key number assigned to headnote ten.

13.   Each headnote is a summary of a point of law from the Court's opinion. Since the headnote is written by a West editor and not a member of the Court, you cannot cite the language of the headnote as precedent. You must cite the language written by the justice in the opinion. Link to or scroll to the part of the opinion where the point of law from headnote ten is discussed. Read the section. What does the Court say a recipient must receive before an individual brings suit under Title IX?

14.   *The Bluebook* requires citing an opinion of the United States Supreme Court to the official reports (U.S.), if available. Star paging enables attorneys using Westlaw to cite to the *United States Reports* (U.S.) paging without using U.S. itself. On Westlaw, page numbers preceded by one asterisk indicate the *United States Reports* (U.S.) pages and page numbers preceded by two asterisks indicate *Supreme Court Reporter* (S. Ct.) pages. Looking at the case on Westlaw and using star paging, state the page of *United States Reports* (U.S.) on which the corresponding material related to the tenth **[10]** West headnote begins. **Hint**: You may need to scroll up until you see the number preceded by one asterisk.

15.   On what page of the *Supreme Court Reporter* (S. Ct.) do you find the actual opinion that discusses the point of law from the tenth [10] West headnote? **Hint**: Remember to use the asterisks as your guide.

16.   Question 8 asked you about the **disposition** of the case, that is, how the Supreme Court treated the judgment of the court below. The **holding** is another part of a case, the application of rules of law to the specific key facts in the case. Did the Court hold that the private right of action implied by Title IX encompasses claims of retaliation? You may want to review the syllabus of the case.

17.   Where in the United States Code can you find Title XI of the Education Amendments of 1972 codified?

SUPREME COURT REPORTERS AND PARTS OF A CASE
EXERCISE D

GOALS OF THIS ASSIGNMENT:
To familiarize you with the parts of a case on LexisNexis.
To introduce you to star paging.

CITATION RULES: Use *The Bluebook: A Uniform System of Citation*, 18th ed., Rules 10.2, 10.2.1, 10.2.2, 10.3.1, 10.3.2, 10.4, 10.5, 18, and tables T.1, T.6, and T.10. Use the format for court documents and legal memoranda and assume that the case citation appears in a citation sentence.

Sign onto LexisNexis at http://www.lexisnexis.com/lawschool and use Get a Document to retrieve 424 U.S. 295.

1.   What is the case name? Use correct form (Rule 10.2).

2.   On what date was the case decided?

3.   What is the docket number of the case?

4.   Which party is the petitioner?

5.   Which Justice wrote the opinion of the court?

6.   Which Justice wrote a dissenting opinion?

7.   What was the lower court cite of this case, on its way up to the Supreme Court? **Note**: You are looking for the cite of an F.2d case.

8.   How did the Supreme Court act on the judgment of the court below?

9.   Who argued the cause for the petitioner?

10.   You found this case on LexisNexis using its official *United States Reports* cite. Notice that LexisNexis provides you with the citations to several other unofficial versions including the *Supreme Court Reporter* (S. Ct.), published by West, and the *U.S. Supreme Court Reports–Lawyers' Edition* (L. Ed. 2d), published then by Lawyers Co-operative Publishing Company and now by LexisNexis. These two reporters are unofficial reporters for United States Supreme Court cases.

      a.   What is the S. Ct. cite?

      b.   What is the L. Ed. 2d cite?

11.   The LexisNexis editors add headnotes to the beginning of each case. The editors write a headnote, or summary, for each key legal point of a case. In addition, you will see the headnotes that editors wrote for the print version found in *U.S. Supreme Court Reports–Lawyers' Edition*. How many LexisNexis headnotes have the editors written for this case?

12.   The LexisNexis editors assign topics to each headnote. State the complete topic from the first LexisNexis headnote.

13. Each headnote is a summary of a key legal point of the Court's opinion. Since the headnote is written by a LexisNexis editor and not a member of the Court, you cannot cite the language of the headnote as precedent. You must cite the language written by the justice in the opinion. Link or scroll to the part of the opinion where the point of law from headnote one is discussed. Read the section. For what purpose does the Court say specified sections of every township in the proposed State were granted to Arizona?

14. *The Bluebook* requires citing an opinion of the United States Supreme Court to the official reports (U.S.), if available. Star paging enables attorneys using LexisNexis to cite to the *United States Reports* (U.S.) paging without using U.S. itself. On LexisNexis, page numbers preceded by one asterisk indicate the *United States Reports* (U.S.) pages, page numbers preceded by two asterisks indicate *Supreme Court Reporter* (S. Ct.) pages, and page numbers preceded by three asterisks indicate *U.S. Supreme Court Reports–Lawyers' Edition* (L. Ed. 2d) pages. Looking at the case on LexisNexis and using star paging, state the page of *United States Reports* (U.S.) on which the corresponding material related to the first LexisNexis headnote begins. **Hint**: You may need to scroll up until you see the number preceded by one asterisk.

15. On what page of the *U.S. Supreme Court Report–Lawyers' Edition* (L. Ed. 2d) do you find the actual opinion that discusses the legal point from the first LexisNexis headnote? **Hint**: Remember to use the asterisks as your guide.

16. Question 8 asked you about the **disposition** of the case, that is, how the Supreme Court treated the judgment of the court below. The **holding** is another part of a case, the application of rules of law to the specific key facts in the case. Did the Court hold that one issue for remand was whether, under state law and the provisions of the lease, petitioner could not possess a compensable leasehold interest upon the federal condemnation?

17. Which U.S. Constitutional provision provides for just compensation for land taken by condemnation?

ASSIGNMENT THREE
REGIONAL REPORTER CASES
EXERCISE A

GOALS OF THIS ASSIGNMENT:
To acquaint you with the Table of Cases in the digests.
To compare the features of regional reporters.

CITATION RULES: For this assignment when citing a case, assume you are citing the case in a legal document that will be submitted to a state court that does not require parallel cites.

Assume you want to find the unofficial (West reporter or regional) text of *Bicknese v. Sutula*, a 2003 Supreme Court of Wisconsin case. When you know the case name and jurisdiction, but do not know the citation, one way to find the citation is to look it up in a digest table of cases. Look up *Bicknese v. Sutula* in the Table of Cases volume in either *West's Wisconsin Key Number Digest*, the *North Western Digest 2d*, or the *Eleventh Decennial Digest, Part 2*.

1. What is the full citation of the case? (Remember, this means name, cite, jurisdiction, court and year according to Rule 10 of *The Bluebook*.)

Find the unofficial report of the case in the *North Western Reporter* and answer Questions 2-8.

2. Notice the long, one-paragraph summary of the facts and holding. This is called the synopsis and West editors wrote it. According to the synopsis, how did the Supreme Court dispose of the decision of the Court of Appeals?

3. Notice the headnotes (one-sentence summaries of points of law). All headnotes in the regional reporters that follow West topic and key numbers are written by West editors. How many headnotes are listed here?

4. A topic and key number precede each headnote in a regional reporter, like those you saw in Assignment Two. What is the topic and key number for the ninth headnote?

Never quote from or cite to the synopsis or headnotes. You can, however, search them on WESTLAW, along with the topics and key numbers. Cases are divided into different parts, called **fields** on WESTLAW and **segments** on LEXIS. Fields and segments can be searched separately, or with the rest of the case.

5. Remember, you can find the part of the opinion that corresponds to the ninth headnote by looking for the corresponding boldface number in brackets in the opinion. On what page of the opinion do you find the corresponding text for the ninth headnote?

6. Read the opinion. Did the court hold that Sutula was not entitled to public officer immunity because in making the job offer to Bicknese, he was under a ministerial duty to correctly set the terms of the offer?

7. Look at the beginning of the case. What is the cite to the official reports, which is given just above the name of the case?

8. Look at the title page of the *North Western Reporter* volume. List **five** states covered in the *North Western Reporter.*

9. Using your textbook or *The Bluebook: A Uniform System of Citation*, state the regional reporters in which the following states' cases are found:

        a. Arkansas

        b. Illinois

        c. West Virginia

In this assignment, you used the table of cases in a digest to find the cite to a case. You then found that case in a regional reporter. Does your own state have an official reporter? Check table T.1 in *The Bluebook* or ask your instructor.

ASSIGNMENT THREE
REGIONAL REPORTER CASES
EXERCISE B

GOALS OF THIS ASSIGNMENT:
To acquaint you with the Table of Cases in the digests.
To compare the features of regional reporters.

CITATION RULES: For this assignment when citing a case, assume you are citing the case in a legal document that will be submitted to a state court that does not require parallel cites.

Assume you want to find the unofficial (West reporter or regional) text of *Cornelius v. Crosby*, a 1979 Supreme Court of Georgia case. When you know the case name and jurisdiction, but do not know the citation, one way to find the citation is to look it up in a digest table of cases. Look up *Cornelius v. Crosby* in the Table of Cases volume in either the *Georgia Digest 2d*, the *South Eastern Digest 2d* or the *Ninth Decennial Digest, Part 1*.

1.   What is the full citation of the case?   (Remember, this means name, cite, jurisdiction, court and year according to Rule 10 of *The Bluebook*.)

Find the unofficial report of the case in the *South Eastern Reporter* and answer Questions 2-8.

2.   Notice the long, one-paragraph summary of the facts and holding. This is called the synopsis and West editors wrote it. According to the synopsis, how did the Supreme Court dispose of the decision of the Superior Court?

3.   Notice the headnotes (one-sentence summaries of points of law). All headnotes in the regional reporters that follow West topic and key numbers are written by West editors. How many headnotes are listed here?

4.   A topic and key number precede each headnote in a regional reporter, like those you saw in Assignment Two. What is the topic and key number for the sixth headnote?

Never quote from or cite to the synopsis or headnotes. You can, however, search them on WESTLAW, along with the topics and key numbers. Cases are divided into different parts, called **fields** on WESTLAW and **segments** on LEXIS. Fields and segments can be searched separately, or with the rest of the case.

5.   Remember, you can find the part of the opinion that corresponds to the ninth headnote by looking for the corresponding boldface number in brackets in the opinion. On what page of the opinion do you find the corresponding text for the sixth headnote?

6.   Read the opinion. Did the court indicate it was necessary that the testator declare the instrument he executed to be his will?

7.   Look at the beginning of the case. What is the citation to the official reports, which is given just above the name of the case?

8.   Look at the title page of a *South Eastern Reporter* volume. List the **five** states covered in the *South Eastern Reporter.*

9.   Using your textbook or *The Bluebook: A Uniform System of Citation*, state the regional reporters in which the following states' cases are found:

        a. Connecticut

        b. Kansas

        c. Tennessee

In this assignment, you used the table of cases in a digest to find the cite to a case. You then found that case in a regional reporter. Does your own state have an official reporter? Check table T.1 in *The Bluebook* or ask your instructor.

ASSIGNMENT THREE
REGIONAL REPORTER CASES
EXERCISE C

GOALS OF THIS ASSIGNMENT:
To acquaint you with the Title field search on Westlaw.
To compare the features of regional reporters.

CITATION RULES: For this assignment when citing a case, assume you are citing the case in a legal document that will be submitted to a state court that does not require parallel cites.

> **Sign on to Westlaw at http://lawschool.westlaw.com.**
>
> Assume you want to find the unofficial (West reporter or regional) text of *Barrett v. Montesano*, a 2004 Supreme Court of Connecticut case. When you know the case name and jurisdiction, but do not know the citation, one way to find the citation is to use the Title field search on Westlaw. Select the Connecticut state cases database, **CT-CS**. You can access this database by one of two ways: 1) start in the main directory and link to the following sequence **U.S. State Materials > Case Law > Individual State & Other U.S. Jurisdictions > Connecticut**; or 2) type "**CT-CS**" in the "**Search for a database**" box. In the search box, you can search just the names of the cases in the database by using the Title field search. For example, the search **TI(Smith & Jones)** will pull up all cases in the database where Smith and Jones are parties. Use the Title field search and look up *Barrett v. Montesano*. **Note**: This search is parallel to using a print digest's Table of Cases to find the citation to a case when you know only the name of the case.

1.   What is the full citation of the case? (Remember, this means name, cite, jurisdiction, court and year according to Rule 10 of *The Bluebook*.)

> **Scroll through the unofficial report of the case from the *Atlantic Reporter 2d* on Westlaw and answer Questions 2-8.**

2.   Notice the background and holding at the beginning of the opinion. This is called the synopsis and West editors wrote it. According to the synopsis, how did the Supreme Court dispose of the decision of the Superior Court?

3.   Notice the headnotes (one-sentence summaries of points of law). All headnotes in the regional reporters that follow West topic and key numbers are written by West editors. How many headnotes are listed here?

4.   A topic and key number precede each headnote in a published case on Westlaw, like those you saw in Assignment Two. On Westlaw, you see the full analysis for the topic and key number. The analysis includes the topic, its assigned topic number, and then there is a "k" standing for key number, with the last portion of the number being the key number that appears in the digest. Therefore, you must look at the last line of the topic/key number analysis for the topic and key number assigned to the headnote. What is the topic and key number for the seventeenth headnote?

Never quote from or cite to the synopsis or headnotes. You can, however, search them on WESTLAW, along with the topics and key numbers. Cases are divided into different parts, called **fields** on WESTLAW. You can run a search in a database where you limit the search to look only at the fields of a case that you specify. You can search the synopsis using the synopsis (**SY**) field, the digest topic and key number using the topic (**TO**) field, the headnote summary paragraph using the headnote (**HE**) field, and both the topic and headnote using the digest (**DI**) field.

Once you have found a case of interest, you can limit the text that is displayed only to the fields you select to view. To do so, click on the **Tools** drop-down on the bottom right. Select **Limit by Fields** and click **GO**. You now see a list of Westlaw fields. You can select fields including Synopsis, Backgound, Holding, Digest, Topic, and Headnote among others. Once you make your selection and click OK, only the fields you have selected will display.

5.   Remember, you can link to the part of the opinion that corresponds to the seventeenth headnote by clicking on the bracketed headnote number. On what page of the *Atlantic Reporter 2d* version of the opinion do you find the corresponding text for the seventeenth headnote? Remember star paging from Assignment Two. **Hint**: Remember to use the asterisks as your guide.

6. Read the opinion. According to the court, when does the limitation period for actions in negligence begin to run?

7. Look at the beginning of the case. What is the official cite, which is given in the header as well as at the beginning of the case?

8. One of the nice features included in cases on Westlaw that is not included in the reporter version is the ability to see what subtopic the key number represents. Look at headnote six. What subtopic under topic "Statutes" does key number 190 stand for?

9. Using you textbook or *The Bluebook: A Uniform System of Citation*, state the regional reporters in which the following states' cases are found:

    a. California

    b. Iowa

    c. Vermont

    In this assignment, you used the Title field search on Westlaw to find a case when you knew the case name and its jurisdiction. Does your own state have an official reporter? Check table T.1 in *The Bluebook* or ask your instructor.

ASSIGNMENT THREE
REGIONAL REPORTER CASES
EXERCISE D

GOALS OF THIS ASSIGNMENT:
To acquaint you with the Name segment search on LexisNexis.
To compare the features of regional reporters.

CITATION RULES: For this assignment when citing a case, assume you are citing the case in a legal document that will be submitted to a state court that does not require parallel cites.

> **Sign on to LexisNexis at <ins>http://www.lexisnexis.com/lawschool</ins>.**

> Assume you want to find the unofficial (West reporter or regional) text of *Hetzel v. Clarkin*, a 1989 Supreme Court of Kansas case. When you know the case name and jurisdiction, but do not know the citation, one way to find the citation is to use the Name segment search on LexisNexis. Select the source for Kansas state cases, **Legal > State Legal-U.S. > Kansas > Find Cases > KS State Cases, Combined.** In the search box, you can search just the names of the cases in the source by using the Name segment search. For example, the search **NAME(Smith & Jones)** will pull up all cases in the source where Smith and Jones are parties. Use the Name segment search and look up *Hetzel v. Clarkin*. **Note**: This search is parallel to using a print digest's Table of Cases to find the citation to a case when you know only the name of the case.

1. What is the full citation of the case? (Remember, this means name, cite, jurisdiction, court and year according to Rule 10 of *The Bluebook*.)

Scroll through the case on LexisNexis and answer Questions 2-8.

2. Notice the gray box with the procedural posture and the overview of the case. This is called the case summary and LexisNexis editors wrote it. According to the case summary, how did the Supreme Court of Kansas dispose of the decision of the district court?

3. Notice the headnotes (short summaries of points of law). LexisNexis headnotes are written by LexisNexis editors. How many headnotes are listed here?

4. Each LexisNexis headnote is assigned at least one topic and sometimes more than one topic. What is the first topic for the second LexisNexis headnote?

    Never quote from or cite to the case summary or headnotes. You can, however, search them on LexisNexis. Cases are divided into different parts, called **segments** on LexisNexis. You can run a search in a source where you limit the search to look only at the segments of a case that you specify. You can search the case summary using the LN-SUMMARY segment and you can search the LexisNexis headnotes using the LN-HEADNOTES segment.

    Once you have found a case of interest, you can navigate to particular point in the case by using the **Explore** feature. To do so, click on the **Explore** button on the bottom left. A list of parts will display. Click on the part that you want to read. You are taken directly to that part of the case. You can select parts of the case including case summary, overview, outcome, and LexisNexis headnotes among others. Once you make your selection and click OK, only the fields you have selected will display.

5. Remember, you can link to the part of the opinion that corresponds to the ninth headnote by clicking on the headnote number. On what page of the *Pacific Reporter* version of the opinion do you find the corresponding text for the second headnote? Remember star paging from Assignment Two. Hint: Remember to use the asterisks as your guide.

6. Read the opinion. Did the court hold that Supreme Court Rule 7.07(b) is not applicable to the party appealing?

7. Look at the beginning of the case. What is the official cite, which is given in the header as well as at the beginning of the case?

8.   One of the nice features of the LexisNexis headnotes is the ability to explore the legal topics online. Look at the topic for the second headnote. Click on "Insurance Law" link in the first topic. Examine the subtopics under Insurance Law. What is the related topic for Claims & Contracts?

9.   Using your textbook or *The Bluebook: A Uniform System of Citation*, state the regional reporters in which the following states' cases are found:

        a. Colorado

        b. New Hampshire

        c. Virginia

In this assignment, you used the Name segment search on LexisNexis to find a case when you knew the case name and its jurisdiction. Note: You can also use the Get a Document by Party Name template when you know the name of a case. Does your own state have an official reporter? Check table T.1 in *The Bluebook* or ask your instructor.

ASSIGNMENT FOUR
FINDING CASES BY SUBJECT
EXERCISE A

GOALS OF THIS ASSIGNMENT:
To introduce you to finding cases by subject in the West digests.
To give you practice at the various methods of using digests.

CITATION RULES: For this assignment when citing a case, assume you are citing the case in a legal document that will be submitted to a state court that does not require parallel cites.

Please research federal copyright cases for the Second Circuit. We need to know whether or not a sculpture that was a "work made for hire" and installed in a New York City commercial building may be altered by the building's owner. Another attorney has given you a relevant case, *Carter v. Helmsley-Spear, Inc.*, a 1995 United States Court of Appeals, Second Circuit case which has a headnote on point. Use this case to find other relevant cases. This is called the "one good case" approach. Check the Table of Cases in either 1) the *West's Federal Practice Digest 4th* or 2) the *Tenth Decennial Digest, Part 2* (in that order of preference) to find the West reporter cite for the case.

1. What is the West reporter cite for the case?

2. Look up the case in the regional reporter. The relevant headnote for our issue is headnote twelve. What is the West topic and key number of headnote twelve?

3. We now have a West topic and key number to begin our digest research. First, let's find out just what this topic and key number represent. Find the analysis outline at the very beginning of the topic from Question 2 in your digest. Examine the list of key numbers. What does the key number from Question 2 stand for? Include all relevant topics of which your key number may be a subtopic.

You will be using the same digest to answer Questions 4-11a or 4-11b.

4. Go to your key number and look at the cases listed under it. Is there another United States Court of Appeals, Second Circuit case arising out of New York from 1992 digested under this topic and key number? If so, provide the full West reporter citation of the case according to Rule 10 of *The Bluebook*. **TIP**: You will need to look up the subsequent case to obtain its date for your citation.

5. Now you will use the topic approach. The topic approach merely involves reading the list of key numbers at the beginning of the topic (the topic outline) and looking for relevant key numbers. Go back to the topic outline (called "Analysis") for **Copyrights and Intellectual Property**. If you were looking for cases concerning the transfer of a copyright upon death, under what topic and key number would you look?

6. Look up that key number. State the name as listed of the 1992 United States Court of Appeals, Second Circuit case arising out of New York that involves the illegitimate daughter of a singer composer.

7. Now you will use the keyword approach. Look in the Descriptive Word Index volumes (either at the beginning or the end of the set). Using the descriptive word approach, find the topic and key number for cases dealing with copyright of musical compositions. To what topic and key number are you referred?

8. Look up the topic and key number and find a 2000 United States Court of Appeals, Second Circuit case arising out of New York. List the full West reporter citation of the case in correct form.

SECTION I: Complete Questions 9a-13a in Section I if you used *West's Federal Practice Digest 4th* for this assignment.

HOW TO UPDATE YOUR DIGEST RESEARCH IF YOU ARE USING *WEST'S FEDERAL PRACTICE DIGEST 4TH*:

Step 1. Current digest volumes are supplemented by annual pocket parts. Look in the pocket part for your topic and key number.
OR
If the pocket part is too thick to fit in the volume, the pocket part becomes a free standing pamphlet that updates that particular volume. Look in the pamphlet for your topic and key number.

Step 2. Depending on how recently the annual pocket parts were issued, your digest may have a pamphlet that directly supplements the annual pocket parts. If so, look up your topic and key number in this pamphlet.

Step 3. If the digest has a supplemental pamphlet from Step 2, check the "Closing with Cases Reported in" section on the second page of the pamphlet. If there is not a supplemental pamphlet, check the "Closing with Cases Reported in" section on the second page of the pocket part/pamphlet from Step 1.

Step 4. Go the reporter volume that you identified in Step 3. Beginning with the volume listed in the "Closing with Cases Reported in" from Step 3, look in the digest sections in the back of all bound volumes and in the front of all advance sheets to see if any recent cases have appeared under your topic and key number.

9a. Does your digest volume have a pocket part or pamphlet as explained in Step 1? If so, look up the topic and key number from Question 7. Are there any cases from the United States Court of Appeals, Second Circuit digested under this topic and key number?

10a. Does your digest have a supplemental pamphlet as explained in Step 2? If so, look up the topic and key number from Question 7. Are there any cases from the United States Court of Appeals, Second Circuit digested under this topic and key number?

11a. Perform Step 3 of updating the digest by looking at the "Closing with Cases Reported in" statement on the second page of the supplemental pamphlet for the digest if there are any. If not, look at the "Closing with Cases Reported in" on the second page of the pocket part/pamphlet. According to the "Closing with Cases Reported in," what is the last volume of F.3d that the digest pocket part/pamphlet covers?

Now go to the *Federal Reporter 3d* and find the volume from Question 11a.

12a. Each bound reporter volume has a small digest section in the back which gives you the topics and key numbers for the cases printed in that volume. Normally, you would check the digest sections of all of the bound reporters beginning with the volume from Question 11a. For this assignment, however, check **only** the **most recent** bound volume. Are there any United States Court of Appeals, Second Circuit cases digested under your topic and key number?

13a. Now check the *Federal Reporter's* advance sheets. Bound volumes are updated by paperbound advance sheets. Several advance sheets are bound together into a reporter. In advance sheets, the digest section is in the front, just before the decisions begin. Normally, you would look at the digest section in all of the advance sheets for your topic and key number. For this assignment, however, check **only** the **most recent** advance sheet. Are there any United States Court of Appeals, Second Circuit cases are digested under your topic and key number?

SECTION II: Complete Questions 9b-13b in Section II if you used a Decennial Digest for this assignment.

HOW TO UPDATE YOUR DIGEST RESEARCH IF YOU ARE USING A DECENNIAL DIGEST:

Step 1. **Look for your topic and key number in all of the subsequent Decennial Digests that were issued after the one you used in this assignment.**

Step 2. **The most recent Decennial Digest is updated by the General Digest. You will need to look at every volume of the General Digest for your topic and key number.**

Step 3.   **Check the "Closing with Cases Reported in" on the second page of the last General Digest on the shelf.**

Step 4.   **Go the reporter volume that you identified in Step 3. Beginning with the volume listed in the "Closing with Cases Reported in" from Step 3, look in the digest sections in the back of all bound volumes and in the front of all advance sheets to see if any recent cases have appeared under your topic and key number.**

9b.   Are there any subsequent Decennial Digests since the Decennial Digest you used in this exercise? If so, look up the topic and key number from Question 7 in each subsequent Decennial Digest. Are there any cases from the United States Court of Appeals, Second Circuit digested under this topic and key number?

10b.   Find the General Digests. Look up the topic and key number from Question 7 in each volume of the General Digest. Are there any cases from the United States Court of Appeals, Second Circuit digested under this topic and key number?

11b.   Perform Step 3 of updating the digest by looking at the "Closing with Cases Reported in" statement on the second page of the last General Digest on the shelf. According to the "Closing with Cases Reported in," what is the last volume of F.3d that this volume of the General Digest covers?

Now go to the *Federal Reporter 3d* and find the volume from Question 11b.

12b.   Each bound reporter volume has a small digest section in the back which gives you the topics and key numbers for the cases printed in that volume. Normally, you would check the digest sections of all of the bound reporters beginning with the volume from Question 11b. For this assignment, however, check **only** the **most recent** bound volume. Are there any United States Court of Appeals, Second Circuit cases digested under your topic and key number?

13b. Now check the *Federal Reporter's* advance sheets. Bound volumes are updated by paperbound advance sheets. Several advance sheets are bound together into a reporter. In advance sheets, the digest section is in the front, just before the decisions begin. Normally, you would look at the digest section in all of the advance sheets for your topic and key number. For this assignment, however, check **only** the **most recent** advance sheet. Are there any United States Court of Appeals, Second Circuit cases digested under your topic and key number?

One great advantage of the West topic and key number system is that you can use it for **all jurisdictions**. The same topic and key number can be used for researching all state and federal courts whose decisions are published in West reporters. Different West digests will group jurisdictions in different ways.

Regional digests contain state cases from each state covered by that particular region. The federal digests cover all of the federal courts, and the Decennial and General Digests, all of the state and federal jurisdictions. Use the most appropriate digest in your library, and provide the full citation, in correct form, for the following case. Search under the topic and key number from **Question 2**.

14. Check the *Illinois Digest 2d* or the *Tenth Decennial Digest, Part 2*. Provide the full regional citation, in correct form, of the 1984 Appellate Court of Illinois case digested under the topic and key number from Question 2.

ASSIGNMENT FOUR
FINDING CASES BY SUBJECT
EXERCISE B

GOALS OF THIS ASSIGNMENT:
To introduce you to finding cases by subject in the West digests.
To give you practice at the various methods of using digests.

CITATION RULES: For this assignment when citing a case, assume you are citing the case in a legal document that will be submitted to a state court that does not require parallel cites.

Please research federal cases for the Seventh Circuit. We need to investigate whether an adult relative other than a spouse may give consent to search a defendant's residence in Illinois. Another attorney has given you a relevant case, *United States v. Chaidez*, a 1990 United States Court of Appeals, Seventh Circuit case which has a headnote on point. Use this case to find other relevant cases. This is called the "one good case" approach. Check the Table of Cases in either 1) the *West's Federal Practice Digest 4th* or 2) the *Tenth Decennial Digest, Part 1* (in that order of preference) to find the West reporter cite for the case.

1.   What is the West reporter cite for the case?

2.   Look up the case in the West reporter reporter. The relevant headnote for our issue is headnote eight. What is the West topic and key number of headnote eight?

3.   We now have a West topic and key number to begin our digest research. First, let's find out just what this topic and key number represent. Find the analysis outline at the very beginning of the topic from Question 2 in your digest. Examine the list of key numbers. What does the key number from Question 2 stand for? Include all relevant topics of which your key number may be a subtopic.

You will be using the same digest to answer Questions 4-11a or 4-11b.

4.   Go to your key number and look at the cases listed under it. Is there a United States Court of Appeals, Seventh Circuit case arising out of Illinois from 1997 digested under this topic and key number? If so, provide the full West reporter citation of the case according to Rule 10 of *The Bluebook*.

5.   Now you will use the topic approach. The topic approach merely involves reading the list of key numbers at the beginning of the topic (the topic outline) and looking for relevant key numbers. Go back to the topic outline (called "Analysis") for **Searches and Seizures**. If you were looking for cases that discuss landlords or tenants giving consent to search, under what topic and key number would you look?

6.   Look up that key number. State the name as listed of the 1998 United States Court of Appeals, Seventh Circuit case arising out of Illinois that involves a lessee giving consent to search a bedroom.

7.   Now you will use the keyword approach. Look in the Descriptive Word Index volumes (either at the beginning or the end of the set). Using the descriptive word approach, find the topic and key number for cases concerning the withdrawal of consent to a search. To what topic and key number are you referred?

8.   Look up the topic and key number and find the 1996 United States Court of Appeals, Seventh Circuit case arising out of Illinois that discusses that consent may be withdrawn or limited by a criminal suspect. List the full West reporter citation of the case in correct form.

SECTION I: Complete Questions 9a-13a in Section I if you used *West's Federal Practice Digest 4th* for this assignment.

HOW TO UPDATE YOUR DIGEST RESEARCH IF YOU ARE USING *WEST'S FEDERAL PRACTICE DIGEST 4TH:*

Step 1.   Current digest volumes are supplemented by annual pocket parts. Look in the pocket part for your topic and key number.
           OR
           If the pocket part is too thick to fit in the volume, the pocket part becomes a free standing pamphlet that updates that particular volume. Look in the pamphlet for your topic and key number.

Step 2.   Depending on how recently the annual pocket parts were issued, your digest may have a pamphlet that directly supplements the annual pocket parts. If so, look up your topic and key number in this pamphlet.

Step 3.   If the digest has a supplemental pamphlet from Step 2, check the "Closing with Cases Reported in" section on the second page of the pamphlet. If there is not a supplemental pamphlet, check the "Closing with Cases Reported in" section on the second page of the pocket part/pamphlet from Step 1.

Step 4.   Go the reporter volume that you identified in Step 3. Beginning with the volume listed in the "Closing with Cases Reported in" from Step 3, look in the digest sections in the back of all bound volumes and in the front of all advance sheets to see if any recent cases have appeared under your topic and key number.

9a.   Does your digest volume have a pocket part or pamphlet as explained in Step 1? If so, look up the topic and key number from Question 7. Are there any cases from the United States Court of Appeals, Seventh Circuit digested under this topic and key number?

10a.   Does your digest have a supplemental pamphlet as explained in Step 2? If so, look up the topic and key number from Question 7. Are there any cases from the United States Court of Appeals, Seventh Circuit digested under this topic and key number?

11a. Perform Step 3 of updating the digest by looking at the "Closing with Cases Reported in" statement on the second page of the supplemental pamphlet for the digest if there are any. If not, look at the "Closing with Cases Reported in" on the second page of the pocket part/pamphlet. According to the "Closing with Cases Reported in," what is the last volume of F.3d that the digest pocket part/pamphlet covers?

Now go to the *Federal Reporter 3d* and find the volume from Question 11a.

12a. Each bound reporter volume has a small digest section in the back which gives you the topics and key numbers for the cases printed in that volume. Normally, you would check the digest sections of all of the bound reporters beginning with the volume from Question 11a. For this assignment, however, check **only** the **most recent** bound volume. Are there any United States Court of Appeals, Seventh Circuit cases digested under your topic and key number?

13a. Now check the *Federal Reporter's* advance sheets. Bound volumes are updated by paperbound advance sheets. Several advance sheets are bound together into a reporter. In advance sheets, the digest section is in the front, just before the decisions begin. Normally, you would look at the digest section in all of the advance sheets for your topic and key number. For this assignment, however, check **only** the **most recent** advance sheet. Are there any United States Court of Appeals, Seventh Circuit cases are digested under your topic and key number?

SECTION II: Complete Questions 9b-13b in Section II if you used a Decennial Digest for this assignment.

HOW TO UPDATE YOUR DIGEST RESEARCH IF YOU ARE USING A DECENNIAL DIGEST:

Step 1. Look for your topic and key number in all of the subsequent Decennial Digests that were issued after the one you used in this assignment.

Step 2. The most recent Decennial Digest is updated by the General Digest. You will need to look at every volume of the General Digest for your topic and key number.

Step 3. Check the "Closing with Cases Reported in" on the second page of the last General Digest on the shelf.

Step 4. Go the reporter volume that you identified in Step 3. Beginning with the volume listed in the "Closing with Cases Reported in" from Step 3, look in the digest sections in the back of all bound volumes and in the front of all advance sheets to see if any recent cases have appeared under your topic and key number.

9b. Are there any subsequent Decennial Digests since the Decennial Digest you used in this exercise? If so, look up the topic and key number from Question 7 in each subsequent Decennial Digest. Are there any cases from the United States Court of Appeals, Seventh Circuit digested under this topic and key number?

10b. Find the General Digests. Look up the topic and key number from Question 7 in each volume of the General Digest. Are there any cases from the United States Court of Appeals, Seventh Circuit digested under this topic and key number?

11b. Perform Step 3 of updating the digest by looking at the "Closing with Cases Reported in" statement on the second page of the last General Digest on the shelf. According to the "Closing with Cases Reported in," what is the last volume of F.3d that this volume of the General Digest covers?

Now go to the *Federal Reporter 3d* and find the volume from Question 11b.

12b. Each bound reporter volume has a small digest section in the back which gives you the topics and key numbers for the cases printed in that volume. Normally, you would check the digest sections of all of the bound reporters beginning with the volume from Question 11b. For this assignment, however, check **only** the **most recent** bound volume. Are there any United States Court of Appeals, Seventh Circuit cases digested under your topic and key number?

13b. Now check the *Federal Reporter's* advance sheets. Bound volumes are updated by paperbound advance sheets. Several advance sheets are bound together into a reporter. In advance sheets, the digest section is in the front, just before the decisions begin. Normally, you would look at the digest section in all of the advance sheets for your topic and key number. For this assignment, however, check **only** the **most recent** advance sheet. Are there any United States Court of Appeals, Seventh Circuit cases digested under your topic and key number?

One great advantage of the West topic and key number system is that you can use it for **all jurisdictions**. The same topic and key number can be used for researching all state and federal courts whose decisions are published in West reporters. Different West digests will group jurisdictions in different ways.

Regional digests contain state cases from each state covered by that particular region. The federal digests cover all of the federal courts, and the Decennial and General Digests, all of the state and federal jurisdictions. Use the most appropriate digest in your library, and provide the full citation, in correct form, for the following case. Search under the topic and key number from **Question 2**.

14. Check the *Texas Digest 2d* or the *Tenth Decennial Digest, Part 1*. Provide the full regional citation, in correct form, of the 1986 Texas Court of Criminal Appeals case digested under the topic and key number from Question 2.

ASSIGNMENT FOUR
FINDING CASES BY SUBJECT
EXERCISE C

GOALS OF THIS ASSIGNMENT:
To introduce you to finding cases by subject on Westlaw.
To give you practice at the various methods of using West's topics and key numbers.

CITATION RULES: For this assignment when citing a case, assume you are citing the case in a legal document that will be submitted to a state court that does not require parallel cites.

Please research federal cases for the Ninth Circuit. We need to know whether under federal law a judge must be disqualified if the judge has a financial interest in the subject matter in controversy. Another attorney has given you a relevant case, *Davis v. Xerox*, a 1987 United States Court of Appeals, Ninth Circuit case which has a headnote on point. Use this case to find other relevant cases. This is called the "one good case" approach. Sign onto Westlaw. Select the **CTA9** database which contains the United States Court of Appeals, Ninth Circuit opinions. You can access this database in one of two ways: 1) start in the main directory and link to the following sequence **U.S. Federal Materials > - Courts of Appeals Cases by Circuit > 9th Circuit**; or 2) type "CTA9" in the **"Search for a database"** box. Conduct a **Title field search** for the *Davis v. Xerox* case. Find our case in the search results. **TIP:** When doing a **Title field search** using party names replace the "v." with an ampersand. **Example: TI(party & party).**

1.   What is the West reporter cite for the case?

2.   Click on the link to the case. The relevant headnote for our issue is headnote one. What is the West topic and key number of headnote one?

3.   We now have a West topic and key number to begin our research for all Ninth Circuit cases with the same topic and key number. First, let's find out just what this topic and key number represent. Look at the topic and key number analysis for headnote one. What does the key number from Question 2 stand for? Include all relevant topics of which your key number may be a subtopic.

4.   Click on the topic number/key number link for headnote 1. This takes you to Westlaw's Custom Digest search page. Custom Digest allows you to find all of the cases that have been assigned a specific topic and key number in a jurisdiction you specify. Select the federal jurisdiction **U.S. Court of Appeals – 9th Circuit**. Run the search. Is there a 1997 United States Court of Appeals, Ninth Circuit case arising out of California with at least one headnote digested under this topic and key number? If so, provide the full West reporter citation of the case according to Rule 10 of *The Bluebook*.

5.   Now you will use the topic approach. The topic approach merely involves reading the list of key numbers and looking for a relevant key number that covers the point of law you are researching. Go back to the Custom Digest page. Click on the **West Key Number Digest** link at the top of the page. You are looking at the alphabetical list of all West topics and key numbers. The list can be expanded to see all of the key number subtopics. Specifically, you are looking at the topic **Judges** and the key numbers under this topic. If you were looking for cases concerning disqualification of a judge when the judge has a relationship to an attorney in the case, under what topic and key number would you look?

6.   Select this topic and key number. Make sure to uncheck any other key numbers that had been selected previously. Click to search. You are now back to the Custom Digest page with your topic and key number selected to search. Select the federal jurisdiction **U.S. Court of Appeals – 9th Circuit**. Run the search. State the name of the 1995 United States Court of Appeals, Ninth Circuit case arising out of California.

7.   Now you will use the keyword approach. With the keyword approach in Westlaw, you first select the database that contains the cases from the jurisdiction you are researching. You are searching for United States Court of Appeals, Ninth Circuit cases so select the **CTA9** database. Use the DIGEST (DI) field search to look for West topics, key numbers, and headnotes containing the keywords from your question: is a federal judge who is a former owner of property in a county required to disqualify himself from hearing a case involving a property owner's action against the same county? What topic and key number are assigned to this specific issue?

8.   What is the proper citation to the 1987 United States Court of Appeals, Ninth Circuit case arising out of California that deals with the issue from Question 7 and has a headnote with the topic and key number from Question 7?

HOW CURRENT IS YOUR DIGEST RESEARCH ON WESTLAW?

When you conduct a topic and key number search in a Westlaw database, your results are as up to date as you would achieve doing your search in the West paper digest and completing all steps to update the digest in paper— digest volume, digest pocket part or pamphlet, digest interim pamphlet, hardbound reporter volumes, and reporter advance sheets.

One great advantage of the West topic and key number system is that you can use it for **all jurisdictions**. The same topic and key number can be used for researching all state and federal courts whose decisions are published in West reporters.

When you already know the topic and key number you want to use in your search, you can bypass the Custom Digest page and run your search from a database search page. First, you need to know the correct formula for creating your search.

Step 1. Determine the topic number for your topic. On Westlaw, the topic number can be seen before each topic assigned to the headnotes of the cases. The number can also be found in the West Key Number Digest Outline on Westlaw. Your search term will begin with this number.
Example: Topic: Adoption   Topic number = 17

Step 2. Insert the letter "k" in your search to stand for "key number" next to your topic number. Do not insert a space between the two.

Step 3. Insert the key number you want to search next to the "k." Do not insert a space between the "k" and the key number.

Your search term formula is: "Topic number + k + Key number"
      Example: Adoption key number 5 (Persons who may adopt)
            Search term = **17k5**

9.   Use the formula above to create your search term for the topic and key number from **Question 2.**

Select the appropriate database to conduct a topic and key number digest search and provide the full citation, in correct form, for the following cases. Search using the topic and key number search term you created in **Question 9**.

10. You want to determine if there are any Georgia state cases that deal with the disqualification of judges who had pecuniary interests through corporate stock ownership. West editors would have assigned these cases the topic and key number from **Question 2**. Search the **GA-CS** (Georgia state cases) database using the search term from **Question 9**. Provide the full regional citation, in correct form, of the 1955 Georgia Supreme Court case in your results.

11. Assume you need to determine if there are any New Hampshire cases dealing with this same topic. Select the **NH-CS** (New Hampshire state cases) database and conduct a search using the search term from Question 9. What is the name of the 1976 Supreme Court of New Hampshire case?

ASSIGNMENT FOUR
FINDING CASES BY SUBJECT
EXERCISE D

GOALS OF THIS ASSIGNMENT:
To introduce you to finding cases by subject on LexisNexis.
To give you practice at the various methods of using LexisNexis topics.

CITATION RULES: For this assignment when citing a case, assume you are citing the case in a legal document that will be submitted to a state court that does not require parallel cites.

Please research federal cases for the Third Circuit. We need to know whether surnames are entitled to trademark protection. Another attorney has given you a relevant case, *Scott Paper Company v. Scott's Liquid Gold, Inc.*, a 1978 United States Court of Appeals, Third Circuit case which has a headnote on point. Use this case to find other relevant cases. This is called the "one good case" approach. Sign onto LexisNexis. Select the **Legal > Cases – U.S. > U.S. Courts of Appeals – By Circuit > 3rd Circuit – US Court of Appeals Cases** source. Conduct a **Name segment search** for the *Scott Paper Company v. Scott's Liquid Gold, Inc.* case. Find our case in the search results. **TIP:** When doing a **Name segment search** using party names replace the "v." with an ampersand. **Example: NAME(party & party).**

1.   What is the West reporter cite for the case?

2.   Scroll through the case and look at the LexisNexis headnotes. The relevant headnote for our issue is headnote six which has been assigned three topics. What is the third topic for headnote six?

3.   We now have a LexisNexis topic to begin our research. First, let's find out just what point of law this topic covers. Click on the link for the fourth part of your answer for Question 2. Then scroll down to find that term in the Legal Topics list. Click on the "i" in front of the term. What does the topic from Question 2 cover?

4.   Go back to our case. Click on the "ALL" icon at the end of our topic to retrieve all headnotes and additional cases on this topic. Select to search **3rd Circuit – US Court of Appeals, District & Bankruptcy Cases, Combined. Run the search and then click on "Show Headnotes Only."** Is there a 1983 United States Court of Appeals, Third Circuit case with at least one headnote assigned the same topic? If so, provide the full West reporter citation of the case according to Rule 10 of *The Bluebook*.

5.   Now you will use the topic approach. The topic approach merely involves reading the list of topics and looking for a relevant topic that covers the point of law you are researching. Go to the Legal Topic Index page by clicking on the **Search** tab at the top and then click on **by Topic or headnote**. Under **Explore Legal Topics**, you are looking at the alphabetical list of LexisNexis topics. The list can be expanded to see all of the subtopics of each topic. Click on **Trademark Law**. You are now looking at the topic **Trademark Law** and its subtopics. If you were looking for cases concerning whether or not the **subject matter** of **telephone numbers** is entitled to trademark protection, under what topic and subtopics would you look?

6.   Click on that topic/subtopic. Under the **Search by Headnote**, select the jurisdiction **3rd Circuit – US Court of Appeals , District & . . .** and run your search. Click on **Show Headnotes Only**. State the name of the 1992 United States Court of Appeals, Third Circuit case listed.

7.   Now you will use the keyword approach. With the keyword approach in LexisNexis, you first select the source that contains the cases from the jurisdiction you are researching. You are searching for United States Court of Appeals, Third Circuit cases so select the **Legal > Cases – U.S. > U.S. Courts of Appeals – By Circuit > 3rd Circuit – US Court of Appeals Cases** source. Use the LN-HEADNOTES segment search to look for headnotes containing the keywords from your question: in trademark cases, does the court look to the **similarity** in **advertising** and **marketing campaigns** to determine the **likelihood** of **confusion**? What topic and subtopics are assigned to this specific issue?

8.   What is the proper citation of the 2004 United States Court of Appeals, Third Circuit case you found in your search? List the full West reporter citation of the case in correct form.

HOW CURRENT IS YOUR DIGEST RESEARCH ON LEXISNEXIS?

When you conduct a topic search in a LexisNexis source, your results are as current as the source file you are using. For example, most LexisNexis sources are updated as soon as LexisNexis receives the case from the court that issued the opinion.

One advantage of the LexisNexis legal topic system is that you can use it for **all jurisdictions**. The same topic/subtopic can be used for researching all state and federal courts whose decisions are included in the LexisNexis system.

Select the appropriate source to conduct a LexisNexis topic search and provide the full citation, in correct form, for the following cases. Search using the topic from **Question 2**.

9.   You want to determine if there are any California state cases that trademark protection of personal names. LexisNexis editors have assigned these cases the topic from **Question 2**. Go to the Topic Index and select the topic from **Question 2**. Under the **Search by Headnote**, select the jurisdiction **CA State Cases, Combined** and run your search. Click on **Show Headnotes Only**. State the name of the 1900 Supreme Court of California case listed.

10.   Assume you need to determine if there are any United States Court of Appeals, Eighth Circuit cases dealing with this same topic. Go back to the page with the option to **Search by Headnote** and change your jurisdiction **to 8th Circuit – US Court of Appeals, District & . . . .** You should still have the topic from **Question 2** selected. Run your search. Click on **Show Headnotes Only**. What is the name of the 1950 United States Court of Appeals, Eighth Circuit case?

GOAL OF THIS ASSIGNMENT:
To teach you how to identify case history and case treatment in a Shepard's entry either in paper, Shepard's on LexisNexis, or Westlaw's KeyCite.

You are researching federal law from the Second Circuit for a brief you are writing. The subject of the brief is copyright law, particularly whether a "work made for hire" and installed in a commercial building may be altered by the building's owner. You have found several cases that you would like to use in your brief but first need to update the cases to verify they are still good law.

SECTION I: Complete Questions 1a-12a in Section I if your library has the Shepard's volumes available in print.

CITATION RULES: When a case cite appears in your answers, use the standard abbreviation for the reporter as found in *The Bluebook: A Uniform System of Citation*, 18th ed. It may differ substantially from the Shepard's abbreviation. Do not include the case name in your answers.

For questions 1a-4a, Sheparize *Carter v. Helmsley-Spear, Inc.*, 71 F.3d 77 (2d Cir. 1995). Find the case in the **bound** *Shepard's Federal Citations* volume that contain cites to it.

1a.   To verify whether or not a case is good law, you must look at the direct history of the case and the negative indirect history. Shepardize the case and look at the direct history. What is the *United States Reports* (U.S.) cite where certiorari was denied?

2a.   Has a United States Court of Appeals, Second Circuit case cited the *Carter* case for *Carter's* headnote 12? **Hint:** Look for a superscript 12 after the reporter abbreviation (F3d). If so, state the cite as listed in Shepard's. Remember, Shepard's in print does not list the first page of the case, but only the actual page that cites your case.

3a.   What is the cite of the Ninth Circuit decision that followed the *Carter* case?

4a.   Have any A.L.R. Fed. annotations cited *Carter*? If so, state the cites to the annotations.

Reshelve Shepard's Citations.

5a.   Look up the case in your answer to Question 2a. Does this case deal with the issue of works made for hire?

Now, you will Shepardize U.S. Supreme Court case *Community for Creative Non-Violence v. Reid*, 490 U.S. 730, 109 S. Ct. 2166, 104 L. Ed. 2d 811. Examine the spine of *Shepard's United States Citations–United States Reports*, Volumes 1.1-1.11 and find the volume in which your case appears to answer Questions 6a-12a.

6a.   How does Shepard's show parallel cites?

7a.   What is the cite of the same case in the federal court of appeals?

8a.   What is the cite of the court of appeals case from the Second Circuit that explained the *Reid* case?

9a.   What is the regional cite of the Indiana decision that cited the *Reid* case?

10a.   What Second Circuit court of appeals case's dissent cited *Reid*?

11a.   State the Shepard's entry for the **third** listed A.L.R. Fed. annotation that cited *Reid*.

12a.   Did the A.L.R. reference in the previous question appear in the annotation or its supplement? If you need help with this question, refer to the preface.

SECTION II: Complete Questions 1b-10b in section II, if your library does NOT have the Shepard's volumes in print but does subscribe to Westlaw.

CITATION RULES: When a case cite appears in your answers, use the standard abbreviation for the reporter as found in *The Bluebook: A Uniform System of Citation*, 18th ed., give the first page of the citing case, and give the pinpoint cite to the page on which the case you are KeyCiting is actually cited. **Example: 100 U.S. 1, 4+.** Do not include the case name in your answers.

> **For questions 1b-5b, KeyCite *Carter v. Helmsley-Spear, Inc.*, 71 F.3d 77 (2d Cir. 1995). Logon to http://lawschool.westlaw.com.**

1b.   To verify whether or not a case is good law, you must look at the direct history of the case and the negative indirect history. KeyCite the case. Look at the **Direct History** section. What is the *United States Reports* (U.S.) cite where certiorari was denied?

> **To see all cases and documents that cite *Carter*, click on the Citing References link on the left.**

2b.   You can limit your display of cases citing *Carter* to cases that cite *Carter* for points of law in *Carter's* West headnotes. What is the West reporter cite of the 2004 United States Court of Appeals, Second Circuit case that cited *Carter* for the point of law in West headnote 12? Click on the **Limit KeyCite Display** link on the bottom. Under **Headnotes**, select headnote 12 (Copyrights k. 41(2)). Click on the **Jurisdiction** arrow on the left. Select **Second Circuit Ct. App.** Click Apply and scroll down to find your result.

3b. Link to the case from Question 2b. Maximize and skim the case. Does this case deal with the issue of works made for hire?

Click your back button to go back to KeyCite. Click on the Cancel Limits link before completing the next question.

4b. What is the West reporter cite of the 2000 Ninth Circuit decision that cited (two stars) the *Carter* case? Click on the **Limit KeyCite Display** link on the bottom. Click on the **Jurisdiction** arrow on the left. Select **Ninth Circuit Ct. App.** Click **Apply** and scroll down to find your result.

Click on the Cancel Limits link before completing the next question.

5b. You are looking for an A.L.R. annotation that cites *Carter*. Click on the **Limit KeyCite Display** link on the bottom. Click on the **Document Type** arrow on the left. Unclick all selections except **ALR annotations**. Click **Apply** and scroll down to find your result. What is the cite of the 1996 A.L.R. Fed. annotation that cites *Carter*?

Now, you will KeyCite a U.S. Supreme Court case *Community for Creative Non-Violence v. Reid*, 490 U.S. 730, 109 S. Ct. 2166, 104 L. Ed. 2d 811. Type the *United States Reports* cite into the KeyCite citation box and click GO.

6b. What KeyCite signal has been assigned to the *Reid* case?

7b. Look at the **Direct History** section. What is the West reporter cite of the same case in the federal court of appeals that reversed the district court?

To see all cases and documents that cite *Reid*, click on the Citing References link on the left.

8b.   What is the West reporter cite of the court of appeals case from the 2002 Second Circuit that discussed (three stars) the *Reid* case? Click on the **Limit KeyCite Display** link on the bottom. Click on the **Jurisdiction** arrow on the left. Select **Second Circuit Ct. App.** Click on the **Depth of Treatment** arrow on the left. Unclick all selections except the three stars for **Discussed**. Click **Apply** and scroll down to find your result.

Click on the Cancel Limits link before completing the next question.

9b.   What is the West reporter cite of the 1995 Indiana decision that cited the *Reid* case? Click on the **Limit KeyCite Display** link on the bottom. Click on the **Jurisdiction** arrow on the left. Select **Indiana** under State Cases. Click **Apply** and scroll down to find your result.

Click on the Cancel Limits link before completing the next question.

10b. What is the West reporter cite for the 2004 Second Circuit court of appeals case whose dissent cited *Reid*? Click on the **Limit KeyCite Display** link on the bottom. Click on the **Locate** arrow on the left. Type "dissent" in the search box. Click on the **Jurisdiction** arrow on the left. Select **Second Circuit Ct. App.** Click on the **Document Type** arrow on the left. Unclick all selections except **Other courts** under Cases. Click **Apply** and scroll down to find your result.

SECTION III: Complete Questions 1c-10c in section III, if your library does NOT have the Shepard's volumes in print but does subscribe to LexisNexis.

CITATION RULES: When a case cite appears in your answers, use the standard abbreviation for the reporter as found in *The Bluebook: A Uniform System of Citation*, 18th ed., give the first page of the citing case, and give the pinpoint cite to the page on which the case you are Shepardizing is actually cited. **Example: 100 U.S. 1, 4.** Do not include the case name in your answers.

For questions 1c-5c, Shepardize *Carter v. Helmsley-Spear, Inc.*, 71 F.3d 77 (2d Cir. 1995). Logon to http://www.lexisnexis.com/lawschool.

1c.   To verify whether or not a case is good law, you must look at the direct history of the case and negative indirect history. Shepardize the case. Scroll down to the **Subsequent Appellate History** section. What is the *United States Reports* (U.S.) cite where certiorari was denied?

2c.   Remember that the LexisNexis online version of the *Carter* opinion has been assigned LexisNexis topics and headnotes. What is the West reporter cite of the 2004 United States Court of Appeals, Second Circuit **reported** case that cited *Carter* for the point of law in LexisNexis headnote 11? Click on the **Focus – Restrict By** link. Under **Jurisdictions available in FULL**, select **2nd Circuit**. Under **Headnotes available in FULL**, select LexisNexis **HN11**. Click **Apply** and scroll down to find your result.

3c.   Link to the case from Question 2c. Does this case deal with the issue of works made for hire?

      Click the Return to *Shepard's* link. Click on the Unrestricted link before completing the next question.

4c.   What is the West reporter cite of the Ninth Circuit decision that followed the *Carter* case? Click on the **Focus – Restrict By** link. Under **Analyses available in FULL**, select **Followed**. Under **Jurisdictions available in FULL**, select **9th Circuit**. Click **Apply** and scroll down to find your result.

      Click on the Unrestricted link before completing the next question.

5c.   You are looking for a law review article that cites *Carter*. Click on the **Focus – Restrict By** link. Under **Jurisdictions available in FULL**, then **Others**, select **Law Reviews**. Click **Apply** and scroll down to find your result. What is the cite of the 2007 California Law Review article that cites *Carter*?

Now, you will Shepardize U.S. Supreme Court case *Community for Creative Non-Violence v. Reid*, 490 U.S. 730, 109 S. Ct. 2166, 104 L. Ed. 2d 811. Type the *United States Reports* cite into the *Shepardize* search box and click GO.

6c.   What Shepard's signal has been assigned to the *Reid* case?

7c.   Look at the **Prior History** section. What is the West reporter cite of the same case in the federal court of appeals that reversed the district court?

8c.   What is the West reporter cite of the court of appeals case from the Second Circuit that explained the *Reid* case? Click on the **Focus – Restrict By** link. Under **Analyses available in FULL**, select **Explained**. Under **Jurisdictions available in FULL**, select **2nd Circuit**. Click **Apply** and scroll down to find your result.

Click on the Unrestricted link before completing the next question.

9c.   What is the West reporter cite of the 1995 Indiana decision that cited the *Reid* case? Click on the **Focus – Restrict By** link. Under **Jurisdictions available in FULL**, select **Indiana**. Click **Apply** and scroll down to find your result.

Click on the Unrestricted link before completing the next question.

10c.   What is the West reporter cite of the 2004 Second Circuit court of appeals case whose dissent cited *Reid*? Click on the **Focus – Restrict By** link. Under **Analyses available in FULL**, select **Dissenting Op.** Under **Jurisdictions available in FULL**, select **2nd Circuit**. Click **Apply** and scroll down to find your result.

ASSIGNMENT FIVE
UPDATING AND VALIDATING CASES–CITATORS
EXERCISE B

GOAL OF THIS ASSIGNMENT:
To teach you how to identify case history and case treatment in a Shepard's entry either in paper, Shepard's on LexisNexis, or Westlaw's KeyCite.

You are researching federal law from the Seventh Circuit for a brief you are writing. The subject of the brief is Fourth Amendment searches, specifically whether an adult relative other than a spouse may give consent to search a defendant's residence. You have found several cases that you would like to use in your brief but first need to update the cases to verify they are still good law.

SECTION I: Complete Questions 1a-12a in Section I if your library has the Shepard's volumes available in print.

CITATION RULES: When a case cite appears in your answers, use the standard abbreviation for the reporter as found in *The Bluebook: A Uniform System of Citation*, 18th ed. It may differ substantially from the Shepard's abbreviation. Do not include the case name in your answers.

For questions 1a-4a, Sheppardize *United States v. Chaidez*, 919 F.2d 1193 (7th Cir. 1990). Find the case in the <u>bound</u> *Shepard's Federal Citations* volume that contain cites to it.

1a.   To verify whether or not a case is good law, you must look at the direct history of the case and the negative indirect history. Shepardize the case. What is the **first** listed *United States Reports* (U.S.) cite where certiorari was denied?

2a.   Have any United States Court of Appeals, Seventh Circuit cases cited the *Chaidez* case for *Chaidez's* headnote 8? **Hint**: Look for a superscript 8 after the reporter abbreviation (F2d or F3d). If so, state the **second** listed cite as listed in Shepard's. Remember, Shepard's in print does not list the first page of the case, but only the actual page that cites your case.

3a.   What is the cite of the United States District Court decision from the Fourth Circuit that followed the *Chaidez* case?

4a.   Has an A.L.R. Fed. annotation cited *Chaidez*? If so, state the cite.

        Reshelve Shepard's Citations.

5a.   Look up the case in your answer to Question 2a. Does this case involve an adult relative giving consent to search?

        Now, you will Shepardize U.S. Supreme Court case *Frazier v. Cupp*, 394 U.S. 731, 89 S. Ct. 1420, 22 L. Ed. 2d 684. Examine the spine of *Shepard's United States Citations–United States Reports*, Volumes 1.1-1.11 and find the volume in which your case appears to answer Questions 6a-12a.

6a.   How does Shepard's show parallel cites?

7a.   What is the cite of the same case in the federal court of appeals?

8a.   What is the cite of the **first** listed court of appeals case from the Seventh Circuit that followed the *Frazier* case?

9a.   What is the West reporter cite of the Mississippi decision that cited the *Frazier* case?

10a.   What Seventh Circuit court of appeals case's dissent cited *Frazier*?

11a.   State the Shepard's entry for the **third** listed A.L.R. Fed. annotation that cited *Frazier*.

12a.   Did the A.L.R. reference in the previous question appear in the annotation or its supplement? If you need help with this question, refer to the preface.

SECTION II: Complete Questions 1b-10b in section II, if your library does NOT have the Shepard's volumes in print but does subscribe to Westlaw.

CITATION RULES: When a case cite appears in your answers, use the standard abbreviation for the reporter as found in *The Bluebook: A Uniform System of Citation*, 18th ed., give the first page of the citing case, and give the pinpoint cite to the page on which the case you are KeyCiting is actually cited. **Example: 100 U.S. 1, 4+.** Do not include the case name in your answers.

> **For questions 1b-5b, KeyCite *United States v. Chaidez*, 919 F.2d 1193 (7th Cir. 1990). Logon to <ins>http://lawschool.westlaw.com</ins>.**

1b.   To verify whether or not a case is good law, you must look at is the direct history of the case and the negative indirect history. KeyCite the case. Look at the **Direct History** section. What is the *United States Reports* (U.S.) cite where certiorari was denied on June 24, 1991?

> **To see all cases and documents that cite *Chaidez*, click on the Citing References link on the left.**

2b.   You can limit your display of cases citing *Chaidez* to cases that cite *Chaidez* for points of law in *Chaidez's* West headnotes. What is the West reporter cite of the 1998 United States Court of Appeals, Seventh Circuit case that cited *Chaidez* for the point of law in West headnote 8? Click on the **Limit KeyCite Display** link on the bottom. Under **Headnotes**, select headnote 8 (Search and S k. 178). Click on the **Jurisdiction** arrow on the left. Select **Seventh Circuit Ct. App.** Click Apply and scroll down to find your result.

3b.   Link to the case from Question 2b. Does this case involve an adult relative giving consent to search?

Click your back button to go back to KeyCite. Click on the Cancel Limits link before completing the next question.

4b.   What is the cite of the 2006 Fourth Circuit, United States District Court decision out of Virginia that cited (two stars) the *Chaidez* case?   Click on the **Limit KeyCite Display** link on the bottom. Click on the **Jurisdiction** arrow on the left. Select **Virginia** under **Fourth Circuit Ct. App.**   Click **Apply** and find your result.

Click on the Cancel Limits link before completing the next question.

5b.   You are looking for an A.L.R. annotation that cites *Chaidez*. Click on the **Limit KeyCite Display** link on the bottom. Click on the **Document Type** arrow on the left. Unclick all selections except **ALR annotations**. Click **Apply** and find your result. What is the cite of the 2000 A.L.R. Fed. annotation that cites *Chaidez*?

Now, you will KeyCite U.S. Supreme Court case *Frazier v. Cupp*, 394 U.S. 731, 89 S. Ct. 1420, 22 L. Ed. 2d 684. Type the *United States Reports* cite into the KeyCite citation box and click GO.

6b.   What KeyCite signal has been assigned to the *Frazier* case?

7b.   Look at the **Direct History** section. What is the West reporter cite of the same case in the federal court of appeals?

To see all cases and documents that cite *Frazier*, click on the Citing References link on the left.

8b.   What is the cite of the 1974 court of appeals case from the Seventh Circuit that cited (two stars) the *Frazier* case? Click on the **Limit KeyCite Display** link on the bottom. Click on the **Jurisdiction** arrow on the left. Select **Seventh Circuit Ct. App.** Click on the **Depth of Treatment** arrow on the left. Unclick all selections except the two stars for **Cited**. Click **Apply** and scroll down to find your result.

Click on the Cancel Limits link before completing the next question.

9b.   What is the West reporter cite of the 1989 Mississippi decision that cited the *Frazier* case? Click on the **Limit KeyCite Display** link on the bottom. Click on the **Jurisdiction** arrow on the left. Select **Mississippi** under State Cases. Click **Apply** and find your result.

Click on the Cancel Limits link before completing the next question.

10b.   What 1973 Seventh Circuit court of appeals case's dissent cited *Frazier*? Click on the **Limit KeyCite Display** link on the bottom. Click on the **Jurisdiction** arrow on the left. Select **Seventh Circuit Ct. App.** Click on the **Locate** arrow on the left. Type "dissent" in the search box. Click on the **Document Type** arrow on the left. Unclick all selections except **Other courts** under Cases. Click **Apply** and scroll down to find your result.

SECTION III: Complete Questions 1c-10c in section III, if your library does NOT have the Shepard's volumes in print but does subscribe to LexisNexis.

CITATION RULES: When a case cite appears in your answers, use the standard abbreviation for the reporter as found in *The Bluebook: A Uniform System of Citation*, 18th ed., give the first page of the citing case, and give the pinpoint cite to the page on which the case you are Shepardizing is actually cited. **Example: 100 U.S. 1, 4.** Do not include the case name in your answers.

In questions 1c-5c, Shepardize *United States v. Chaidez*, 919 F.2d 1193 (7th Cir. 1990). Logon to <u>http://www.lexisnexis.com/lawschool</u>.

1c.   To verify whether or not a case is good law, you must look at the direct history of the case and negative indirect history. Shepardize the case. Scroll down to the **Subsequent Appellate History** section. What is the **first** listed *United States Reports* (U.S.) cite where certiorari was denied?

2c.   Remember that the LexisNexis online version of the *Chaidez* opinion has been assigned LexisNexis topics and headnotes. What is the West reporter cite of the 1998 United States Court of Appeals, Seventh Circuit decision that cited *Chaidez* for the point of law in LexisNexis headnote 23? Click on the **Focus – Restrict By** link. Under **Jurisdictions available in FULL**, select **7th Circuit**. Under **Headnotes available in FULL**, select LexisNexis **HN23**. Click **Apply** and scroll down to find your result.

3c.   Link to the case from Question 2c. Does this case involve an adult relative giving consent to search?

        Click the Return to *Shepard's* link. Click on the Unrestricted link before completing the next question.

4c.   What is the West reporter cite of the 2006 Fourth Circuit, United States District Court decision that followed the *Chaidez* case? Click on the **Focus – Restrict By** link. Under **Analyses available in FULL**, select **Followed**. Under **Jurisdictions available in FULL**, select **4th Circuit**. Click **Apply** and scroll down to find your result.

        Click on the Unrestricted link before completing the next question.

5c.   You are looking for a law review article that cites *Chaidez*. Click on the **Focus – Restrict By** link. Under **Jurisdictions available in FULL**, then **Others**, select **Law Reviews**. Click **Apply** and scroll down to find your result. What is the cite of the 2000 Cardozo Law Review article that cites *Chaidez*?

Now, you will Shepardize U.S. Supreme Court case *Frazier v. Cupp*, 394 U.S. 731, 89 S. Ct. 1420, 22 L. Ed. 2d 684. Type the *United States Reports* cite into the *Shepardize* search box and click GO.

6c.   What Shepard's signal has been assigned to the *Frazier* case?

7c.   Look at the **Case History** section. What is the West reporter cite of the same case in the federal court of appeals?

8c.   What is the West reporter cite of the 1974 court of appeals case from the Seventh Circuit that followed the *Frazier* case? Click on the **Focus – Restrict By** link. Under **Analyses available in FULL**, select **Followed**. Under **Jurisdictions available in FULL**, select **7th Circuit**. Click **Apply** and scroll down to find your result.

Click on the Unrestricted link before completing the next question.

9c.   What is the West reporter cite of the 1989 Mississippi decision that cited the *Frazier* case? Click on the **Focus – Restrict By** link. Under **Jurisdictions available in FULL**, select **Mississippi**. Click **Apply** and scroll down to find your result.

Click on the Unrestricted link before completing the next question.

10c.   What is the West reporter cite to the 1973 Seventh Circuit court of appeals case whose dissent cited *Frazier*? Click on the **Focus – Restrict By** link. Under **Analyses available in FULL**, select **Dissenting Op.** Under **Jurisdictions available in FULL**, select **7th Circuit**. Click **Apply** and scroll down to find your result.

ASSIGNMENT FIVE
UPDATING AND VALIDATING CASES–CITATORS
EXERCISE C

GOAL OF THIS ASSIGNMENT:
To teach you how to identify case history and case treatment in Westlaw's KeyCite.

> **You are researching federal law from the Ninth Circuit for a brief you are writing. The subject of the brief deals with whether a judge will be disqualified if the judge has a financial interest in the subject matter in controversy. You have found several cases that you would like to use in your brief but first need to update the cases to verify they are still good law.**

CITATION RULES: When a case cite appears in your answers, use the standard abbreviation for the reporter as found in *The Bluebook: A Uniform System of Citation*, 18th ed. It may differ substantially from the Shepard's abbreviation. Do not include the case name in your answers.

> **For questions 1-5, KeyCite *Davis v. Xerox*, 811 F.2d 1293 (9th Cir. 1987). Logon to http://lawschool.westlaw.com.**

1.   To verify whether or not a case is good law, you must look at the direct history of the case and the negative indirect history. KeyCite the case. Look at the **Direct History** section. What is the *United States Reports* (U.S.) cite where certiorari was denied?

2.   Look at the **Negative Citing References** section. Are there any cases from the Ninth Circuit?

> **To see all cases and documents that cite *Davis*, click on the Citing References link on the left.**

3.   You can limit your display of cases citing *Davis* to cases that cite *Davis* for points of law in *Davis's* West headnotes. What is the cite of the 1987 United States Court of Appeals, Ninth Circuit case that cited *Davis* for the point of law in West headnote 1? Click on the **Limit KeyCite Display** link on the bottom. Under **Headnotes**, select headnote 1 (Judges k. 43). Click on the **Jurisdiction** arrow on the left. Select **Ninth Circuit Ct. App.** Click **Apply** and find your result.

4.   Link to the case from Question 3. Maximize and read the case. Does this case address the issue of when a judge must be disqualified for having a pecuniary interest in a case over which the judge is presiding?

     Click your back button to go back to KeyCite. Click on the Cancel Limits link before completing the next question.

5.   You are looking for an A.L.R. annotation that cites *Davis*. Click on the **Limit KeyCite Display** link on the bottom. Click on the **Document Type** arrow on the left. Unclick all selections except **ALR annotations**. Click **Apply** and find your result. What is the cite of the 2000 A.L.R. Fed. annotation that cites *Davis*?

     Now, you will KeyCite U.S. Supreme Court case *Rooker v. Fidelity Trust Co.*, 263 U.S. 413, 44 S. Ct. 149, 68 L. Ed. 362. Type the *United States Reports* cite into the KeyCite citation box and click GO.

6.   What KeyCite signal has been assigned to the *Rooker* case?

7.   Look at the **Negative Citing References** section. What is the cite of the 1994 Ninth Circuit decision that declined to extend *Rooker*?

     To see all cases and documents that cite *Rooker*, click on the Citing References link on the left.

8.   What is the West reporter cite of the 2005 court of appeals case from the Ninth Circuit that examined (four stars) the *Rooker* case? Click on the **Limit KeyCite Display** link on the bottom. Click on the **Jurisdiction** arrow on the left. Select **Ninth Circuit Ct. App.** Click on the **Depth of Treatment** arrow on the left. Unclick all selections except the four stars for **Examined**. Click **Apply** and scroll down to find your result.

Click on the Cancel Limits link before completing the next question.

9.   What is the West reporter cite of the 2006 Alaska decision that cited the *Rooker* case? Click on the **Limit KeyCite Display** link on the bottom. Click on the **Jurisdiction** arrow on the left. Select **Alaska** under States Cases. Click **Apply** and find your result.

Click on the Cancel Limits link before completing the next question.

10.   What is the *United States Reports* (U.S.) cite of the 1997 decision whose dissent cited *Rooker*? Click on the **Limit KeyCite Display** link on the bottom. Click on the **Locate** arrow on the left. Type "dissent" in the search box. Click on the **Jurisdiction** arrow on the left. Select **U.S. Supreme Court.** Click on the **Document Type** arrow on the left. Unclick all selections except **Highest Courts** under Cases. Click **Apply** and scroll down to find your result.

Westlaw's Table of Authorities feature allows you to retrieve a list of all of the cases cited in your case.

11.   Retrieve the Table of Authorities for the *Rooker* case by clicking on the **Table of Authorities** link towards the bottom of the left-hand frame. How many cases were cited in *Rooker*?

ASSIGNMENT FIVE
UPDATING AND VALIDATING CASES–CITATORS
EXERCISE D

GOAL OF THIS ASSIGNMENT:
To teach you how to identify case history and case treatment in Shepard's on LexisNexis.

You are researching federal law from the Third Circuit for a brief you are writing. The subject of the brief deals with whether or not surnames are entitled to trademark protection. You have found several cases that you would like to use in your brief but first need to update the cases to verify they are still good law.

CITATION RULES: When a case cite appears in your answers, use the standard abbreviation for the reporter as found in *The Bluebook: A Uniform System of Citation*, 18th ed. It may differ substantially from the Shepard's abbreviation. Do not include the case name in your answers.

For questions 1-5, Shepardize *Scott Paper Co. v. Scott's Liquid Gold, Inc.*, **589 F.2d 1225 (3d Cir. 1978).** Logon to http://www.lexisnexis.com/lawschool.

1. To verify whether or not a case is good law, you must look at the direct history of the case and negative indirect history. Shepardize the case. Look at the **Unrestricted** *Shepard's* **Summary** box. Is there any **Subsequent Appellate History** for this case?

2. Retrieve the negative indirect history cases by clicking on the **All Neg** link. What is the West reporter cite for the 1987 Third Circuit opinion that questioned *Scott*?

Click on the Unrestricted link before completing the next question.

3. Remember that the LexisNexis online version of the *Scott* opinion has been assigned LexisNexis topics and headnotes. What is the cite of the 2004 United States Court of Appeals, Third Circuit decision that cited *Scott* for the point of law in LexisNexis headnote 6? Click on the **Focus – Restrict By** link. Under **Jurisdictions available in FULL**, select **3rd Circuit**. Under **Headnotes available in FULL**, select LexisNexis **HN6**. Click **Apply** and scroll down to find your result.

4.   Link to the case from Question 3. Does this case discuss trademark protection of a name?

Click the Return to *Shepard's* link. Click on the Unrestricted link before completing the next question.

5.   You are looking for a law review article that cites *Scott*. Click on the **Focus – Restrict By** link. Under **Jurisdictions available in FULL**, then **Others**, select **Law Reviews**. Click **Apply** and scroll down to find your result. What is the cite of the 1985 Iowa Law Review article that cites *Scott*?

Now, you will Shepardize U.S. Supreme Court case *Two Pesos, Inc. v. Taco Cabana, Inc.*, 505 U.S. 763, 112 S. Ct. 2753, 120 L. Ed. 2d 615. Type the *United States Reports* cite into the *Shepardize* search box and click GO.

6.   What Shepard's signal has been assigned to the *Two Pesos* case?

7.   Look at the **Prior History** section. What is the West reporter cite of the same case in the federal court of appeals that affirmed the district court?

8.   Retrieve the negative indirect history cases by clicking on the **All Neg** link. What is the West reporter cite for the 1994 Third Circuit opinion that distinguished *Two Pesos*?

Click on the Unrestricted link before completing the next question.

9.   What is the West reporter cite of the 1997 New Jersey decision that cited the *Two Pesos* case? Click on the **Focus – Restrict By** link. Under **Jurisdictions available in FULL**, select **New Jersey**. Click **Apply** and scroll down to find your result.

Click on the Unrestricted link before completing the next question.

10.   What is the West reporter cite of the 2003 Fourth Circuit court of appeals case whose dissent cited *Two Pesos*? Click on the **Focus – Restrict By** link. Under **Analyses available in FULL**, select **Dissenting Op.**   Under **Jurisdictions available in FULL**, select **4th Circuit**. Click **Apply** and scroll down to find your result.

LexisNexis's Table of Authorities feature allows you to retrieve a list of all of the cases cited in your case.

11.   Retrieve the Table of Authorities for the *Two Pesos* case by clicking on the **TOA** link located after the case cite in the header. How many cases were cited in *Two Pesos*?

ASSIGNMENT SIX
AMERICAN LAW REPORTS
EXERCISE A

GOALS OF THIS ASSIGNMENT:
To give you practice at using the A.L.R. tables and indexes.
To find whether a relevant annotation has been superseded or supplemented.

You are researching federal copyright law. You have learned that a "work made for hire" is a work prepared by an employee within the scope of his or her employment. In addition, some commissioned works may be "works for hire" if there is a written agreement. If the "work is made for hire," the employer or the person who ordered the work is the initial copyright owner, not the employee. You now need to determine whether a "work made for hire" and installed in a commercial building may be altered by the building's owner under the Copyright Act of 1976. Use the Index to A.L.R. to find a relevant A.L.R. Fed. annotation by subject.

1. What is the cite to the A.L.R. Fed. annotation?

Find the annotation from 132 A.L.R. Fed. and answer Questions 2-10.

2. What is the correct citation of the annotation itself? (See Rule 16.6.6 of *The Bluebook*.)

3. Remember, the full text of an opinion accompanies each annotation that explains the law in the case's subject area. This case is referenced at the bottom of the first page of the annotation. State the full West reporter citation of the opinion whose text is printed in full. Use proper *Bluebook* form.

4. Go back to the annotation. To which sections of the Am. Jur. 2d topic *Copyright and Literary Property* could you turn to find related material?

5. Examine the Index section. Which section discusses art works?

6. Examine the Table of Cases. This table will quickly tell you all jurisdictions covered by the annotation. Are any Second Circuit cases discussed in this annotation?

7. Examine the scope notes and the references to related matters in the Preliminary Matters section. State the cite of the annotation listed which discusses the copyrightability of sculptural works.

8. Examine § 11[a]. What 1995 Second Circuit case is cited in this section? State its name.

9. Look at the beginning of the annotation in the pocket part to this volume. Examine the beginning of the updating material for a note telling you that the annotation has been superseded. Is there a note telling you that this annotation has been superseded?

10. The pocket parts in A.L.R.3d, 4th, 5th, 6th, Fed., and Fed. 2d volumes also provide information on later cases that are relevant to the annotation. Provide the full West reporter citation of a 2000 District of Delaware case that updates § 11[a] of the annotation.

   Reshelve A.L.R. and find the last volume of the A.L.R. Index.

11. You can also tell if an annotation has been superseded by looking in the Annotation History Table, found at the end of the last A.L.R. Index volume and its pocket part. Has 183 A.L.R. Fed. been superseded? If so, state the cite of the superseding annotation.

ASSIGNMENT SIX
AMERICAN LAW REPORTS
EXERCISE B

GOALS OF THIS ASSIGNMENT:
To give you practice at using the A.L.R. tables and indexes.
To find whether a relevant annotation has been superseded or supplemented.

___

You are researching federal law to determine whether an adult relative other than a spouse may give consent to search a defendant's residence under the Fourth Amendment. Use the Index to A.L.R. to find a relevant A.L.R. Fed. annotation by subject.

1.   What is the cite to the A.L.R. Fed. annotation?

Find the annotation from 160 A.L.R. Fed. and answer Questions 2-10.

2.   What is the correct citation of the annotation itself?   (See Rule 16.6.6 of *The Bluebook*.)

3.   Remember, the full text of an opinion accompanies each annotation that explains the law in the case's subject area. This case is referenced at the bottom of the first page of the annotation. State the full West reporter citation of the opinion whose text is printed in full. Use proper *Bluebook* form.

4.   Go back to the annotation. To which sections of the Am. Jur. 2d topic *Searches and Seizures* could you turn to find related material?

5.   Examine the Index section.   Which section discusses an adult child giving consent?

6.   Examine the Table of Cases.   This table will quickly tell you all jurisdictions covered by the annotation. Are any Seventh cases discussed in this annotation?

7.   Examine the scope notes and the references to related matters in the Preliminary Matters section. State the cite of the annotation listed which discusses the validity of requirement that, as a condition of probation, defendant submit to warrantless searches.

8.   Examine § 6[a]. What 1990 Seventh Circuit case is cited in this section? State its name.

9.   Look up the cite to the annotation in the pocket part to this volume. Examine the beginning of the updating material for a note telling you that the annotation has been superseded.   Is there a note telling you that this annotation has been superseded?

10.   The pocket parts in A.L.R.3d, 4th, 5th, 6th, Fed., and Fed. 2d volumes also provide information on later cases that are relevant to the annotation. Provide the full regional citation of a 2007 federal district court case that updates § 8[a] of the annotation.

Reshelve A.L.R. and find the last volume of the A.L.R. Index.

11.   You can also tell if an annotation has been superseded by looking in the Annotation History Table, found at the end of the last A.L.R. Index volume and its pocket part. Has 92 A.L.R. Fed. 25 been superseded? If so, state the cite of the superseding annotation.

ASSIGNMENT SIX
AMERICAN LAW REPORTS
EXERCISE C

GOALS OF THIS ASSIGNMENT:
To give you practice finding an A.L.R. on Westlaw.
To find whether a relevant annotation has been superseded or supplemented.

You are researching federal law to determine whether a judge will be disqualified if the judge has a financial interest in the court matter over which the judge is presiding.

Sign onto Westlaw and select the A.L.R. database, **ALR**. You can access this database in one of two ways: 1) start in the main directory and link to the following sequence **Forms, Treatises, CLEs and Other Practice Material > American Law Reports > American Law Reports**; or 2) type "**ALR**" in the "**Search for a database**" box. In the search box, enter the keywords for your search.

1. What is the cite to the A.L.R. Fed. annotation?

Click on the link to the 163 A.L.R. Fed. and answer Questions 2-10.

2. What is the correct citation of the annotation itself **in print**? (See Rule 16.6.6 of *The Bluebook*.) **Note**: Westlaw provides the copyright date of the print volume in the "originally published" parenthetical.

3. Read the first paragraph of the annotation. This annotation was inspired by a federal decision dealing with the same subject matter. The opinion can be found in a West reporter and in the same volume as your annotation. State the full West reporter citation of the Fifth Circuit opinion whose text is printed in full in the same print A.L.R. volume.

ASSIGNMENT SIX, EXERCISE C, PAGE 2 OF 3

4. Scroll down and click on the **Research References** link. Scroll down to the Legal Encyclopedia section. To which sections of the Am. Jur. 2d topic *Federal Courts* could you turn to find related material?

5. Scroll back up to the Index section. Examine the Index section. Which section discusses a family member owning vehicle manufactured by defendant?

6. Examine the Table of Cases, Laws, and Rules. This table will quickly tell you all jurisdictions covered by the annotation. Are any Ninth Circuit cases discussed in this annotation?

7. Click on the **Research References** link and scroll to the A.L.R. Library section that lists related annotations. State the cite of the annotation listed whose subject is the timeliness of affidavit of disqualification of a trial judge under 28 U.S.C.A. § 144.

8. Examine § 6. What 1987 United States Court of Appeals, Ninth Circuit case is cited in this section? State its name.

9. In this online version of the annotation, information from the pocket part or cumulative supplement is added at the end of each section. This information includes later cases that are relevant to the annotation. Look at the Cumulative Supplement for § 15. Provide the full West reporter citation of the 2004 Eleventh Circuit case that updates § 15 of the annotation.

10. Look at the beginning of your A.L.R. annotation. According to the note, how frequently are the A.L.R. databases updated with relevant new cases?

11. The ALR database on Westlaw contains electronic annotations (e-annos). These annotations are not available in print and are identified by a citation that uses the year for the volume number and the number of the annotation for that year as the page number. **Example: 2007 A.L.R.6th 1.** Go to your **Find this document by citation** box and **Find** 2007 A.L.R.6th 2. What is the title of this annotation?

12. You can also tell if an annotation has been superseded by looking at the note below the author's name or by looking for a KeyCite red flag. Has the electronic annotation from Question 11 (2007A.L.R.6th 2) been superseded? If so, state the cite of the superseding annotation.

ASSIGNMENT SEVEN
REVIEW—FINDING, CITING, AND UPDATING CASES
EXERCISE A

GOALS OF THIS ASSIGNMENT:
To review the use of digests, citators in print or online, and A.L.R. to find cases.
To combine several steps of a research strategy using different types of materials.

Georgia Davis, one of the partners in the criminal defense firm for which you are working as a summer associate in Little Rock, Arkansas, asked you to conduct research for one of her cases. The firm's client, Janet Myers, has been charged with one count each of mail fraud, using a fictitious name or false name to carry on a scheme to defraud by mail, and possessing stolen mail. The government claims Janet stole a credit card application from her neighbor's mailbox, fraudulently applied for the credit card under the neighbor's name, and made 42 charges on the credit card. Janet denies the claims and says that it was her roommate Beverley Anderson who committed the offenses. Attorney Davis tells you that a handwriting expert is on the witness list to testify for the government in this case and has asked you to research the cases that deal with the **admissibility** of a **handwriting expert's testimony** in **federal criminal cases**. Please research federal case law to determine how the court may deal with this situation. Before you begin, identify the federal jurisdiction that includes Arkansas and determine which courts' cases will be mandatory authority in that jurisdiction.

1. If you are unfamiliar with a topic and looking for citations to primary authority for your jurisdiction, a good place to begin your research is in the A.L.R. Go to the A.L.R. Index and look for an A.L.R. Fed. annotation that may help you research this issue. What is the cite to the annotation? **TIP:** The pocket part to the Index volume contains more recent annotations.

Find the 183 A.L.R. Fed. annotation.

2. What is the correct citation of the annotation itself? (See Rule 16.6.6 of *The Bluebook*.)

3.   In section 4[b], does this annotation provide you with a cite to a 2000 United States Court of Appeals Eighth Circuit arising case? If so, provide the full West reporter citation in correct format.

Find the case from Question 3 and read it.

4.   Given your fact situation, is this case on point?

5.   Is a United States Court of Appeals, Eighth Circuit case that is still good law mandatory or persuasive authority if cited to a federal district court in Arkansas?

6.   Look at the headnotes of this case. Several headnotes are relevant to your issue. Which headnote discusses that a handwriting comparison expert's testimony was admissible since it provided the jury knowledge beyond their own and enhanced their understanding of the evidence? List its number, e.g., first, second, third, etc.

7.   What is the topic and key number of this headnote?

8.   Read the opinion corresponding to the point of law for the above headnote. According to this opinion, what is the name of the 1999 United States Court of Appeals, Eleventh Circuit case relied on to find the district court did not abuse its discretion in finding the handwriting expert's testimony to be reliable?

9.   Use *West's Federal Practice Digest 4th* or the *Eleventh Decennial Digest, Part 2* to find other cases that are mandatory authority in your jurisdiction and have been assigned the same relevant topic and key number from Question 7. Provide the full citation in the West reporter for the 2002 United States Court of Appeals, Eighth Circuit case arising out of Arkansas digested under the same topic and key number. **TIP**: The pocket part for the *West's Federal Practice Digest 4th* volume contains more recent cases.

SECTION I: Complete Questions 10a-14a in Section I if your library has the Shepard's volumes available in print.

> You have decided to use the Eighth Circuit case from Question 3 in the memo that you are writing. You must verify that the case is still good law. You can also expand your research to other relevant cases through Shepard's. Shepardize the case in the bound main volume.

10a. Look at the front of the Shepard's at the "History and Treatment Abbreviations" on the inside cover of the volume. Study the abbreviations for the "History of Case." Now find the listing for the cite to your case. Is there any prior or subsequent case history listed?

11a. Turn back to the abbreviations at the front of the volume. Look at the abbreviations under "Treatment of Case." Note that your case has been cited in several other Eighth Circuit cases. As you proceed in your research, you will need to look at these cases to determine if these cases are relevant to your issue. State the **first listed** cite of the case that distinguished your case.

12a. Examine the case listings under the Fourth Circuit. Have any of the cases cited *Jolivet* for the point of law discussed in the sixth headnote? If so, provide the cite of the entry.

> **Look up the case from Question 12a.**

13a. What is the name of the case?

14a. Does the case discuss the issue of the admissibility of testimony of a handwriting expert?

SECTION II: Complete Questions 10b-14b in Section II if your library does NOT have the Shepard's volumes in print but does subscribe to Westlaw.

Logon to http://lawschool.westlaw.com. KeyCite the case from Question 3.

10b. Look at the Direct History for your case. Is there any prior or subsequent history listed?

11b. Look at the cases listed under **Negative Citing References.** What is the cite of the 2004 United States Court of Appeals, Eighth Circuit case that distinguished your case?

12b. Click on **Citing References.** Click on **Limit KeyCite Display.** Check the box for the sixth headnote and click **Apply.** Has a 2002 Eighth Circuit case cited *Jolivet* for the point of law discussed in the sixth headnote? If so, provide the West reporter cite of the entry.

13b. Click on the link for the case from Question 12b. What is the name of the case?

14b. Does the case discuss the issue of the admissibility of testimony of a handwriting expert?

SECTION III: Complete Questions 10c-14c in Section III if your library does NOT have the Shepard's volumes in print but does subscribe to LexisNexis.

> **Logon to http://www.lexisnexis.com/lawschool.** Shepardize the case from Question 3.

10c.   Look at the Shepard's Summary for your case. Is there any prior or subsequent history listed?

11c.   Click on the **All Neg** link at the top. What is the **first listed** cite of the 2004 United States Court of Appeals, Eighth Circuit case that distinguished your case?

Click on the Unrestricted link before completing the next question.

12c.   Click on **FOCUS – Restrict By**. Scroll down to **Headnotes available in FULL**. Check the box for the LexisNexis headnote one (HN1). Click on **Apply**. Has a 2002 Eighth Circuit case cited *Jolivet* for the point of law discussed in the first LexisNexis headnote? If so, provide the cite of the entry.

13c.   Click on the link for the case from Question 12c. What is the name of the case?

14c.   Does the case discuss the issue of the admissibility of testimony of a handwriting expert?

ASSIGNMENT SEVEN
REVIEW—FINDING, CITING, AND UPDATING CASES
EXERCISE B

GOALS OF THIS ASSIGNMENT:
To review the use of digests, citators in print or online, and A.L.R. to find cases.
To combine several steps of a research strategy using different types of materials.

Last week, Mercy Hospital retained the Abernathy law firm in Columbus, Ohio. The hospital is being sued by Julie Kennedy, a former nurse at the hospital. Ms. Kennedy states that her sixteen-year-old son was critically injured in an automobile accident 45 days ago. Two days after the accident, Ms. Kennedy claims she notified the hospital in writing that she would need to take time off to care for her injured son. One week later, the hospital terminated Ms. Kennedy for excessive absenteeism. Ms. Kennedy alleges that Mercy Hospital unlawfully denied her leave under the Family and Medical Leave Act (FMLA). Mercy Hospital states that it was never given notice of a request for leave under the FMLA. You have been asked to research what constitutes adequate **notice** to an **employer** for **leave** under the **federal Family and Medical Leave Act of 1993**. Please research federal case law to determine how the court may deal with this situation. Before you begin, identify the federal jurisdiction that includes Ohio and determine which courts' cases will be mandatory authority in that jurisdiction.

1.   If you are unfamiliar with a topic and looking for citations to primary authority for your jurisdiction, a good place to begin your research is in the A.L.R. Go to the A.L.R. Index and look for an A.L.R. Fed. annotation that may help you research this issue. What is the cite to the annotation? **TIP**: The pocket part to the Index volume contains more recent annotations.

Find the 184 A.L.R. Fed. annotation.

2.   What is the correct citation of the annotation itself? (See Rule 16.6.6 of *The Bluebook*.)

3.   In section 13, does this annotation provide you with a cite to a 1998 United States Court of Appeals Sixth Circuit case? If so, provide the full West reporter citation in correct format.

Find the case from Question 3 and read it.

4.   Given your fact situation, is this case on point?

5.   Is a United States Court of Appeals, Sixth Circuit case that is still good law mandatory or persuasive authority if cited to a federal district court in Ohio?

6.   Look at the headnotes of this case. Several headnotes are relevant to your issue. Which headnote discusses an employee does not need to mention FMLA by name in order to provide employer notice of request but must impart information to employer that is sufficient to reasonably apprise employer of employee's request to leave for a serious health condition? List its number, e.g., first, second, third, etc.

7.   What is the topic and key number of this headnote?

8.   Read the opinion corresponding to the point of law for the above headnote. According to this opinion, what is the name of the 1995 United States Court of Appeals, Fifth Circuit case relied on to support that an employee need only impart information that would reasonably apprise an employer of an employee's request to take time off for a serious health condition?

9.   Use *West's Federal Practice Digest 4th* or the *Eleventh Decennial Digest, Part 2* to find other cases that are mandatory authority in your jurisdiction and have been assigned the same relevant topic and key number from Question 7. Provide the full West reporter citation to the 2004 Sixth Circuit case arising out of Ohio that was digested under the same topic and key number.

SECTION I: Complete Questions 10a-14a in Section I if your library has the Shepard's volumes available in print.

> **You have decided to use the Sixth Circuit case from Question 3 in the memo that you are writing. You must verify that the case is still good law. You can also expand your research to other relevant cases through Shepard's. Shepardize the case in the bound main volumes.**

10a.   Look at the front of the Shepard's at the "History and Treatment Abbreviations" on the inside cover of the volume. Study the abbreviations for the "History of Case." Now find the listing for the cite to your case. Is there any prior or subsequent case history listed?

11a.   Turn back to the abbreviations at the front of the volume. Look at the abbreviations under "Treatment of Case." Note that your case has been cited in several other Sixth Circuit cases. As you proceed in your research, you will need to look at these cases to determine if these cases are relevant to your issue. State the cite of the Sixth Circuit Court of Appeals case that distinguished your case.

12a.   Examine the case listings under the Sixth Circuit. Have any of the cases cited *Brohm* for the point of law discussed in the tenth headnote? If so, provide the **second listed** cite.

> **Look up the case from Question 12a.**

13a.   What is the name of the case?

14a.   Does the case discuss notice under the Family Medical Leave Act?

SECTION II: **Complete Questions 10b-14b in Section II if your library does NOT have the Shepard's volumes in print but does subscribe to Westlaw.**

> Logon to http://lawschool.westlaw.com. KeyCite the case from Question 3.

10b.   Look at the Direct History for your case. Is there any prior or subsequent history listed?

11b.   Look at the cases listed under **Negative Citing References.** What is the West reporter cite of the 2002 United States Court of Appeals, Sixth Circuit case that distinguished your case?

12b.   Click on **Citing References**. Click on **Limit KeyCite Display**. Check the box for the tenth headnote and limit the jurisdiction to the **Sixth Circuit Ct. App.** Click **Apply**. What is the West reporter cite for the Feb. 11, 2005 Sixth Circuit case that cited *Brohm* for the point of law discussed in the tenth headnote?

13b.   Click on the link for the case from Question 12b. What is the name of the case?

14b.   Does the case discuss notice under the Family Medical Leave Act?

SECTION III: **Complete Questions 10c-14c in Section III if your library does NOT have the Shepard's volumes in print but does subscribe to LexisNexis.**

> Logon to http://www.lexisnexis.com/lawschool. Shepardize the case from Question 3.

10c.   Look at the Shepard's Summary for your case. Is there subsequent history listed?

11c.   Click on the **All Neg** link at the top. What is the cite of the 2002 United States Court of Appeals, Sixth Circuit case that distinguished your case?

Click on the Unrestricted link before completing the next question.

12c.   Click on **FOCUS – Restrict By**. Scroll down to **Headnotes available in FULL**. Check the box for the LexisNexis headnote eight (HN8). Click on **Apply**. Has a 2005 Sixth Circuit case arising from Tennessee cited *Brohm* for the point of law discussed in LexisNexis headnote eight? If so, provide the cite of the entry.

13c.   Click on the link for the case from Question 12c. What is the name of the case?

14c.   Does the case discuss notice under the Family Medical Leave Act?

ASSIGNMENT SEVEN
REVIEW—FINDING, CITING, AND UPDATING CASES
EXERCISE C

GOALS OF THIS ASSIGNMENT:
To review the use of Westlaw to find cases using headnotes, KeyCite, and A.L.R.
To combine several steps of a research strategy using different types of materials.

You are working as a summer associate for the Corbin Law Firm in Atlanta, Georgia. Attorney Jason Miller has asked you to conduct research for one of his cases involving client Josef Meister. Mr. Meister came to the United States after World War II and became a naturalized citizen. He faces revocation of his United States citizenship for allegedly serving as a guard at Dachau, a Nazi German concentration camp. Mr. Meister vehemently denies serving as a guard. The Government's case is based, in part, on certain documentation including a Troop Muster Roll from 1944. This document is a standard printed form containing certain biographical information about the guards at Dachau. The information on the document in question appears to identify Mr. Meister. Your assignment is to research whether or not this document will be **admissible** under the **ancient document exception** to the **hearsay** rule under the **Federal Rules of Evidence**. Please research federal case law to determine how the court may treat such a document. Before you begin, identify the federal jurisdiction that includes Georgia and determine which courts' cases will be mandatory authority in that jurisdiction.

Sign on to Westlaw at **http://lawschool.westlaw.com**.

1.   If you are unfamiliar with a topic and looking for citations to primary authority for your jurisdiction, a good place to begin your research is in the A.L.R. Go to the A.L.R. database using **Directory > Forms, Treatises, CLEs and Other Practice Material > American Law Reports > American Law Reports**. Conduct a **Title field search** for an A.L.R. Fed. annotation that may help you research this issue. What is the cite to the annotation?

   Find the 186 A.L.R. Fed. annotation.

2.   What is the correct citation of the annotation itself? (See Rule 16.6.6 of *The Bluebook*.)

3.   Read section 3. What is the first listed 1984 United States Court of Appeals Eleventh Circuit case? Provide the full West reporter citation in correct format.

Click on the link for the case from Question 3 and read it.

4.   Given your fact situation, is this case on point?

5.   Is a United States Court of Appeals, Eleventh Circuit case that is still good law mandatory or persuasive authority if cited to a federal district court in Georgia?

6.   Look at the headnotes of this case. One headnote is relevant to your issue. Which headnote discusses that the Ukrainian police employment forms fell within the ancient document exception to the hearsay rule and were admissible as evidence? List its number, e.g., first, second, third, etc.

7.   What is the topic and key number of this headnote?

8.   Click on the headnote number to jump to the opinion section corresponding to the point of law for the above headnote. Read the section. According to this opinion, the court ruled that the documents fell within the hearsay exception for certain ancient documents. What Federal Rule of Evidence is cited?

9.   Go back to the headnote from Question 6. Click on the **Most Cited Cases** link at the end of the topic. For your jurisdiction, select **Federal** and then **U.S. Federal – 11th Circuit**. Provide the full West reporter citation to the 1961 United States Court of Appeals Fifth Circuit case digested under the same topic and key number. **Note:** Read *Bluebook* Rule 10.8.2 for an explanation of the Fifth Circuit split to create the Eleventh Circuit. This explanation should help you understand why a Fifth Circuit case was retrieved when you selected to search the Eleventh Circuit.

KeyCite the case from Question 3.

10. Look at the Direct History for your case. Is there any prior or subsequent history listed?

11. Look at the cases listed under **Negative Citing References.** What is the West reporter cite of the 1985 United States Court of Appeals, Eleventh Circuit case that distinguished your case?

12. Click on **Citing References**. Click on **Limit KeyCite Display**. Check the box for the sixteenth headnote and click **Apply**. What is the West reporter cite for the 1993 Eastern District of Pennsylvania case that cited *Koziy* for the point of law discussed in the sixteenth headnote?

13. Click on the link for the case from Question 12. What is the name of the case?

14. Does the case mention the ancient document exception to the hearsay rule?

ASSIGNMENT SEVEN
REVIEW—FINDING, CITING, AND UPDATING CASES
EXERCISE D

GOALS OF THIS ASSIGNMENT:
To review the use of LexisNexis to find cases using headnotes and Shepard's.
To combine several steps of a research strategy using different types of materials.

You are working as a summer associate for the law firm of Thomas & Jennings in Pittsburgh, Pennsylvania. Client James Stevens has retained the firm to stop the harassment of a debt collector. Over the past 4 months, Mr. Stevens has received 6 letters and several phone calls from a local attorney, David Barrett. The letters and calls seek payment of a debt Mr. Stevens acknowledges he owes on past due credit cards. The letters are quite obnoxious and degrading to Mr. Stevens. In addition, Mr. Stevens has provided the firm with several recorded messages left on his home voice mail. The messages have a threatening tone and indicate Mr. Stevens's home will be listed for forced sale by the sheriff if Stevens does not immediately pay the debt. The credit card company has hired attorney Barrett to collect this debt. Mr. Barrett engages in debt collection activity on occasion but the majority of his practice involves personal injury. You have been asked to research whether an **attorney** falls within the definition of **"debt collector"** under the **Fair Debt Collection Practices Act**. Please research federal case law to determine how the court may deal with this situation. Before you begin, identify the federal jurisdiction that includes Pennsylvania and determine which courts' cases will be mandatory authority in that jurisdiction.

One place you could begin your research is in the A.L.R. However, the A.L.R. annotations are not available on LexisNexis. As an alternative to the A.L.R., you could also use a secondary source. Let us assume that an attorney in your firm has asked you to help with the research on the case he is working. The attorney has given you a copy of a relevant A.L.R. annotation, 173 A.L.R. Fed. 223. You read the annotation. The cumulative supplement for section 8.5 cites to a case that seems relevant to your research, **396 F.3d 227**.

Sign onto LexisNexis at <u>http://www.lexisnexis.com/lawschool</u>.

1. Use **Get a Document** to retrieve the case found in the A.L.R. Provide the full West reporter citation of the case in correct format.

Read the case from Question 1.

2.   Given your fact situation, is this case on point?
            Yes

3.   Is a United States Court of Appeals, Third Circuit case that is still good law mandatory or persuasive authority if cited to a federal district court in Pennsylvania?

4.   Look at the LexisNexis headnotes of this case. Several headnotes are relevant to your issue. Which headnote discusses that attorneys who regularly engage in debt collection or debt collection litigation are covered by the Fair Debt Collection Practices Act and their litigation activities must comply with the law's requirements? List its number, e.g., first, second, third, etc.

5.   The headnote has been assigned two topics. What is the **second listed** topic of this headnote?

6.   Read the opinion corresponding to the point of law for the above headnote. According to this opinion, what is the citation for the definition of "debt collector" under the Act?

7.   Go back up to the LexisNexis headnote. Click on the **More Like This Headnote** link at the end of the headnote from Question 4. For your jurisdiction, select **US Courts of Appeals** then **3rd Circuit**. Provide the full West reporter citation to the **first listed** 1989 United States Court of Appeals Third Circuit case digested under the same topic and key number.

Shepardize the case from Question 1.

8.   Look at the Shepard's Summary for your case. Is there subsequent history listed?

9.   Click on the **All Neg** link at the top. What is the LexisNexis cite of the Feb. 7, 2008 Eastern District of Pennsylvania case that criticized your case?

Click on the Unrestricted link before completing the next question.

10.   Click on **FOCUS – Restrict By**. Scroll down to **Headnotes available in FULL**. Check the box for the LexisNexis headnote four (HN4). Click on **Apply**. What is the LexisNexis cite of the entry for the Jan. 26, 2007 Eastern District of Pennsylvania case that cited *Piper* for the point of law discussed in LexisNexis headnote four?

11.   Click on the link for the case from Question 10. What is the name of the case?

12.   Does the case discuss that the Fair Debt Collection Practices Act's definition of "debt collector" includes attorneys who regularly engage in debt collection?

ASSIGNMENT EIGHT
FINDING AND CITING STATUTES
EXERCISE A

GOALS OF THIS ASSIGNMENT:
To acquaint you with finding federal and state statutes in your library.
To familiarize you with the rules for citing statutes in *The Bluebook: A Uniform System of Citation*, **18th ed.**

CITATION RULES: You will need to read and apply Rule 12 (including its subsections) and review table T.1 in *The Bluebook*. In this assignment, we give you either a citation or a subject area and you must find federal and state statutes. Once you have found the statutes, you must cite them correctly.

The first three questions require you to find and cite a statute in the official federal code, the *United States Code* (U.S.C.). The citation includes the title number, the code abbreviation, the section number(s), the date of the code appearing on the spine, and the supplement date (if the act appears in the supplement). Include the name of the act or the act's popular name and the original uncodified section of the act if such information would aid in identification. **Example: 23 U.S.C. § 126 (2000 & Supp. V 2005).**

1.   For statutes currently in force, which code should you cite?

2.   Find the U.S.C. in your library.

        a. What is the date of the current edition?

        b. If the code has supplements, what is the date of the latest supplement?

3.   Find and cite the *United States Code*, title 49, sections 44917 to 44921. Update in the latest supplement if needed. Do not include the name of the act.

The next question requires you to find and cite a statute in one of the unofficial federal codes, *United States Code Annotated* (U.S.C.A.). You may cite unofficial codes (U.S.C.A. and U.S.C.S.) when the statute is too recent to appear in the U.S.C. Include the information you used for the U.S.C., in addition to the name of the publisher. You must also include the precise location in either U.S.C.A. or U.S.C.S. where the statute appears. Cite to either the main volume, the pocket part, or both. Since no date appears on the spine of the main volume, the year cited is the copyright date. **Example: 10 U.S.C.A. § 9344 (West 1998 & Supp. 2008).**

4.   Find and cite § 44917 of Title 49 of U.S.C.A. correctly.

Next, you must find and cite a federal session law using *United States Statutes at Large*. According to Rule 12.4 of *The Bluebook*, when citing session laws, always give the name of the statute, the public law number, volume and page number of the Statutes at Large (Stat.), and the year of passage if not revealed in its name. **Example: Home Energy Assistance Act of 1980, Pub. L. No. 96-223, 94 Stat. 288.**

5.   Find and cite 119 Stat. 2550.

For the next two questions, find and cite a state statute in a code. We require that you use the index to find the correct act. When citing a state code, include the name of the code; the chapter, title, or other subdivision; possibly the name of the publisher; and the year of the code. You must use table T.1 to determine proper citation format for individual jurisdictions. **Example: Miss. Code Ann. § 75-5-109 (2004).**

6.   Use the index to the *Florida Statutes Annotated* and find a statute that defines abandoned water wells.

For some states, most notably California, Texas, and New York, include the subject on the spine as part of the name of the code. **Example: Tex. Educ. Code Ann. § 11.058 (Vernon 2006).**

7.   Use the index to the *Annotated California Code* and find a statute that defines affordable rent.

Statutes are online on Westlaw, LexisNexis, and free Internet sites. On Westlaw, you can retrieve statutes if you have the citation with the FIND command. On LexisNexis, use GET A DOCUMENT to locate statutes. The online assignments using Westlaw and LexisNexis follow.

ASSIGNMENT EIGHT
FINDING AND CITING STATUTES
EXERCISE B

GOALS OF THIS ASSIGNMENT:
To acquaint you with finding federal and state statutes in your library.
To familiarize you with the rules for citing statutes in *The Bluebook: A Uniform System of Citation*, 18th ed.

CITATION RULES: You will need to read and apply Rule 12 (including its subsections) and review table T.1 in *The Bluebook*. In this assignment, we give you either a citation or a subject area and you must find federal and state statutes. Once you have found the statutes, you must cite them correctly.

The first three questions require you to find and cite a statute in the official federal code, the *United States Code* (U.S.C.). The citation includes the title number, the code abbreviation, the section number(s), the date of the code appearing on the spine, and the supplement date (if the act appears in the supplement). Include the name of the act or the act's popular name and the original uncodified section of the act if such information would aid in identification. **Example: 23 U.S.C. § 126 (2000 & Supp. V 2005).**

1.   For statutes currently in force, which code should you cite?

2.   Find the U.S.C. in your library.

        a. What is the date of the current edition?

        b. If the code has supplements, what is the date of the latest supplement?

3.   Find and cite the *United States Code*, title 42, sections 11312 to 11316. Update in the latest supplement if needed. Do not include the name of the act.

The next question requires you to find and cite a statute in one of the unofficial federal codes, *United States Code Annotated* (U.S.C.A.). You may cite unofficial codes (U.S.C.A. and U.S.C.S.) when the statute is too recent to appear in the U.S.C. Include the information you used for the U.S.C., in addition to the name of the publisher. You must also include the precise location in either U.S.C.A. or U.S.C.S. where the statute appears. Cite to either the main volume, the pocket part, or both. Since no date appears on the spine of the main volume, the year cited is the copyright date. **Example: 10 U.S.C.A. § 9344 (West 1998 & Supp. 2008).**

4.   Find and cite § 247d-6b of Title 42 of U.S.C.A. correctly.

Next, you must find and cite a federal session law using *United States Statutes at Large*. According to Rule 12.4 of *The Bluebook*, when citing session laws, always give the name of the statute, the public law number, volume and page number of the Statutes at Large (Stat.), and the year of passage if not revealed in its name. **Example: Home Energy Assistance Act of 1980, Pub. L. No. 96-223, 94 Stat. 288.**

5.   Find and cite 117 Stat. 1952.

For the next two questions, find and cite a state statute in a code. We require that you use the index to find the correct act. When citing a state code, include the name of the code; the chapter, title, or other subdivision; possibly the name of the publisher; and the year of the code. You must use table T.1 to determine proper citation format for individual jurisdictions. **Example: Miss. Code Ann. § 75-5-109 (2004).**

6.　Use the index to the *West's Smith-Hurd Illinois Compiled Statutes Annotated* and find the Cannabis Control Act.

For some states, most notably California, Texas and New York, include the subject on the spine as part of the name of the code. **Example: Tex. Educ. Code Ann. § 11.058 (Vernon 2006).**

7.　Use the index to the *Vernon's Texas Statutes and Codes Annotated* published by West and find a statute that on side cowl lights on vehicles.

Statutes are online on Westlaw, LexisNexis, and free Internet sites. On Westlaw, you can retrieve statutes if you have the citation with the FIND command. On LexisNexis, use GET A DOCUMENT to locate statutes. The online assignments using Westlaw and LexisNexis follow.

ASSIGNMENT EIGHT
FINDING AND CITING STATUTES
EXERCISE C

GOALS OF THIS ASSIGNMENT:
To teach you how to find statutes in Westlaw.
To familiarize you with the rules for citing statutes in *The Bluebook: A Uniform System of Citation*, 18th ed.

CITATION RULES: You will need to read and apply Rule 12 (including its subsections) and review table T.1 in *The Bluebook*. In this assignment, we give you either a citation or a subject area and you must find federal and state statutes. Once you have found the statutes, you must cite them correctly. When citing to statutes on Westlaw, refer to Rule 18.1.2.

Sign on to Westlaw at http://lawschool.westlaw.com. On Westlaw, use **Retrieve a Document**, then select **Find**. If there is a print box, do not click the print box. Be careful with printing!

The first question requires you to find and cite a statute in the *United States Code Annotated*. Westlaw retrieves U.S.C.A. The citation includes the title number, the code abbreviation, and the section number(s). The parenthetical includes the name of the publisher if needed, the name of the database, and the currency as given by the database. Include the name of the act or the act's popular name and the original uncodified section of the act if such information would aid in identification. **Click on Currentness** to access the date of the last update. **Example: 23 U.S.C.A. § 126 (West, Westlaw through xxxx).**

1.   Find and cite the *United States Code Annotated*, title 42, section 247d-6. Do not include the name of the act. Refer to Rule 18.1.2, in addition to Rule 12 and table T.1.

Next, you must find and cite a federal session law using *United States Statutes at Large*. According to Rule 12.4 of *The Bluebook*, when citing session laws, always give the name of the statute, the public law number, volume and page number of the Statutes at Large (Stat.), and the year of passage if not revealed in its name. **Example: Home Energy Assistance Act of 1980, Pub. L. No. 96-223, 94 Stat. 288 (Westlaw).**

2.   Find and cite 117 Stat. 1952. Use Rule 18.1.3.

For the next four questions, find and cite state statutes. **Begin with the Directory > U.S. State Materials > Statutes and Legislative Services > Statutes Annotated – Individual States and U.S. Jurisdictions.**

3.   **Select Illinois – Statutes Annotated and then Statutes Index at the top of the Search Page**. Locate in Illinois Statutes – Annotated the Cannabis Control Act. Click on the link to the statute and maximize your viewer box.

4.   **Click back on your browser button. Click on Change Database then select Florida.** Locate in the Florida Statutes Annotated a statute that defines an abandoned water well. Click on the link to the statute and maximize your viewer box.

5.   **Click back on your browser button. Click on Change Database then select California.** Search the index to the California Statutes Annotated and find a statute that defines affordable rent. Click on the link to the statute and maximize your viewer box.

6.   **Click back on your browser button. Click Change Database then select Texas.** Search the index to Texas Statutes - Annotated and find a statute on side cowl lights on vehicles. Click on the link to the statute and maximize your viewer box.

ASSIGNMENT EIGHT
FINDING AND CITING STATUTES
EXERCISE D

GOALS OF THIS ASSIGNMENT:
To teach you how to find statutes in LexisNexis.
To familiarize you with the rules for citing statutes in *The Bluebook: A Uniform System of Citation*, 18th ed.

CITATION RULES: You will need to read and apply Rule 12 (including its subsections) and review table T.1 in *The Bluebook*. In this assignment, we give you either a citation or a subject area and you must find federal and state statutes. Once you have found the statutes, you must cite them correctly. When citing to statutes on LexisNexis, refer to Rule 18.1.2.

Sign on to LexisNexis at http://www.lexisnexis.com/lawschool. On LexisNexis, use **Get a Document.**

The first question requires you to find and cite a statute in the *United States Code Service*. LexisNexis retrieves U.S.C.S. The citation includes the title number, the code abbreviation, the section number(s), the date of the code appearing on the spine, and the supplement date (if the act appears in the supplement). Include the name of the act or the act's popular name and the original uncodified section of the act if such information would aid in identification. The current date of the code section is at the top of the page. **Example: 23 U.S.C.S. § 126 (LexisNexis, LEXIS through xxxx).**

1.   Get and cite the *United States Code Service*, title 42, section 247d-6. Do not include the name of the act. Refer to Rule 18.1.2.

Next, you must find and cite a federal session law using *United States Statutes at Large*. According to Rule 12.4 of *The Bluebook*, when citing session laws, always give the name of the statute, the public law number, volume and page number of the Statutes at Large (Stat.), and the year of passage if not revealed in its name. **Example: Home Energy Assistance Act of 1980, Pub. L. No. 96-223, 94 Stat. 288 (LEXIS).**

2.   Get and cite 117 Stat. 1952. Use Rule 18.1.3.

        For the next four questions, find and cite state statutes. **Click on the Search tab then States Legal – U.S.**

3.   **Search IL – Illinois Compiled Statutes Annotated. Search Table of Contents, use Terms & Connectors, and locate** a statute on cannabis control act. Click on the statute link. Click on Legislative intent.

4.   **Click on Search > States Legal – U.S. > Texas. Search TX- Texas Statutes and Codes Annotated by LexisNexis.** Search in Full-text of source documents (TOC will not work for this search). Locate a statute on fender lamps.

5.   **Click on Search > States Legal – U.S. Search Fl – LexisNexis Florida Annotated Statutes. Search the Full-text of source documents (TOC will not work for this search) and click Terms & Connectors.** Locate in the Florida Statutes Annotated a statute that defines abandoned water wells.

6.   **Click Search > States Legal – U.S. Choose CA – Deering's California Codes Annotated. Search the full text of source documents and click Terms & Connectors.** Locate in the *California Code Annotated* the definition of affordable rent with respect to lower income households. **Note:** Scroll through several citations to find the correct entry.

ASSIGNMENT NINE
FEDERAL CODES AND SESSION LAWS
EXERCISE A

GOALS OF THIS ASSIGNMENT:
To reveal the similarities and differences between the two annotated codes.
To introduce you to federal session laws.
To introduce you to the legislative history materials available in *United States Code Congressional and Administrative News.*

1.   Use the index in U.S.C.A. to find the title and section of the code to answer the following question. Which commission prohibits the use of lead based paint in toys? Answer the question and provide the citation to the code. **Note**: In *The Bluebook*, use Rule 12 and table T.1.

In your research, you will seldom, if ever, use the "official" U.S. Code, because it is not current and does not contain annotations. Therefore to answer Questions 2-7, use the two annotated codes, U.S.C.A. and U.S.C.S., of the code section you found in Question 1. **Be sure to check the pocket parts and the supplementary pamphlets for possible updates!**

2.   Look up the text of the statute from Question 1. Next, look at the information in parentheses at the end of the section. State the date, public law number, and *U.S. Statutes at Large* citation for the 1971 act passed during the 91st Congress.

3.   a.   Which code (U.S.C.A. and/or U.S.C.S.) refers you to the Code of Federal Regulations on Office of Assistant Secretary for Equal Opportunity?
        b.   What is the citation (title and part)?

4.   a.   Which code or codes refers you to ALR Fed?

          b.   List the citation of the ALR Fed provided.

5.   a.   Which code refers you to topic and key numbers in the American Digest System?

          b.   List the **first listed** topic and key number.

6.   a.   Which code refers you to court decisions?

          b.   State the **name** of the 2005 federal district court decision.

7.   a.   Which code refers you to electronic research?

          b.   What system does the code refer you to?

Reshelve the unofficial codes.

Remember that a code is a subject arrangement of current, general laws. Note how helpful the unofficial codes can be since they refer you to cases, encyclopedia articles, law review articles, digests, and secondary materials.

Now, assume that you want to look at the text of 120 Stat. 3372.

To find the text of a law or amendment as Congress passed it, use the *U.S. Statutes at Large* for Questions 8-11.

8.   Find 120 Stat. 3372. Go to the beginning of the Public Law at 120 Stat. 3372. What is the Public Law number?

9.   What is the bill number for the act?

10.   Examine the last page of the act. When was this act approved?

11.   What is the location of this volume in your library (indicate call number, row number, or other location).

Now assume that you wish to see some legislative history for this act. Legislative history refers to committee reports, legislative debates, and hearings generated during the consideration of bills. Courts often consider legislative history when interpreting a statute because legislative history can show legislative intent.

***United States Code Congressional and Administrative News* (U.S.C.C.A.N.) is an accessible source of legislative history and the text of public laws (Questions 12-13).**

12.   The text of the public law you already examined in 120 Stat. 3372 is also reprinted in U.S.C.C.A.N. in 2006, vol. 3. Look it up. Where can you locate the **Legislative History** for the act?

13.   Look up the legislative history (it is in vol. 4). Which Senate Report is reprinted?

ASSIGNMENT NINE
FEDERAL CODES AND SESSION LAWS
EXERCISE B

GOALS OF THIS ASSIGNMENT:
To reveal the similarities and differences between the two annotated codes.
To introduce you to federal session laws.
To introduce you to the legislative history materials available in *United States Code Congressional and Administrative News.*

1. Use the index in U.S.C.A. to find the title and section of the code to answer the following question. What is the prison time for the first violation of a music copyright of a live musical performance and music videos? Answer the question and provide the citation to the code.   **Note**: In *The Bluebook*, use Rule 12 and table T.1.

    In your research, you will seldom, if ever, use the "official" U.S. Code, because it is not current and does not contain annotations. Therefore to answer Questions 2-7, use the two annotated codes, U.S.C.A. and U.S.C.S., of the code section you found in Question 1. **Be sure to check the pocket parts and the supplementary pamphlets for possible updates!**

2. Next, look at the information in parentheses at the end of the section. State the date, public law number, and *U.S. Statutes at Large* citations for the 1997 amendment passed during the 105th Congress.

3. a. Which codes (U.S.C.A. and/or U.S.C.S.) refer you to law review articles?
    b. Who are the authors of the article that appeared in the in 2001?

4.   a.   Which code refers you to the treatise, *Nimmer on Copyright*?
     b.   Which chapter in *Nimmer* addresses rights against bootlegging musical performance?

5.   a.   Which code refers you to topic and key numbers in the American Digest System?
     b.   List the **first listed** topic and key number.

6.   a.   Which code or codes refers you to court decisions?
     b.   State the **name** of the 1999 federal court of appeals decision.

7.   a.   Which code refers you to electronic research?
     b.   What system does the code refer you to?

Reshelve the unofficial codes.

Remember that a code is a subject arrangement of current, general laws. Note how helpful the unofficial codes can be since they refer you to cases, encyclopedia articles, law review articles, digests, and secondary materials.

Now, assume that you want to look at the text of 114 Stat. 644.

To find the text of a law or amendment as Congress passed it, use the *U.S. Statutes at Large* for Questions 8-11.

8. Find 114 Stat. 644. Go to the beginning of the Public Law at 114 Stat. 644. What is the Public Law number?

9. What is the bill number for the act?

10. Examine the last page of the act. When was this act approved?

11. What is the location of this volume in your library (indicate call number, row number, or other location).

Now assume that you wish to see some legislative history for this act. Legislative history refers to committee reports, legislative debates, and hearings generated during the consideration of bills. Courts often consider legislative history when interpreting a statute because legislative history can show legislative intent.

***United States Code Congressional and Administrative News* (U.S.C.C.A.N.) is an accessible source of legislative history and the text of public laws (Questions 12-13).**

12. The text of the public law you already examined in 114 Stat. 644 is also reprinted in U.S.C.C.A.N. in 2000, vol. 1. Look it up. Where can you locate the **Legislative History** for the act?

13. Look up the legislative history (it is in vol. 4). Which Senate Report is reprinted?

ASSIGNMENT NINE
FEDERAL CODES
EXERCISE C

GOALS OF THIS ASSIGNMENT:
To teach you statute searching on Westlaw.
To acquaint you with reading a federal code section on Westlaw.

> **Sign on to Westlaw at http://lawschool.westlaw.com.** These seven questions will ask you to locate a federal code section in U.S.C.A. and then answer questions about the code section.

1. Start in the main Directory. Link to the following sequence: **U.S. Federal Materials > Federal Statutes > United States Code Annotated (U.S.C.A.).** Search for the law on the unauthorized fixation in music videos as an offense. What is the prison time for a first time offense? Use a Terms and Connectors search. Answer the question and provide the citation to the code. In *The Bluebook*, use Rule 18.1.2 and T.1.

2. How current is this section of the code?

3. Scroll to **Historical and Statutory Notes**. Note the references to Senate Reports, House Reports, and reference to U.S. Code Cong. and Adm. News. What is the House Report number for the 1994 act?

4. When you click on the report from Question 3, do you locate a full-text or summary report? Westlaw will first give you a page with links to Part I and Part II of the report. Click on either link.

5.   Click back to the main page of the code section. Under KeyCite, **Proposed Legislation** lists citations to pending bills that reference a statute. Is there proposed legislation for this law? If yes, what year was Senate bill 1749 introduced in the Senate? **Note:** Not all legislation has proposed legislation.

6.   Under KeyCite, click on **Citing References**. Under **Negative Treatments**, what is the name of the case that held a prior version of the code section unconstitutional?

7.   In addition to cases, does KeyCite provide citations to secondary sources?

ASSIGNMENT NINE
FEDERAL CODES
EXERCISE D

GOALS OF THIS ASSIGNMENT:
To teach you statute searching on LexisNexis.
To acquaint you with reading a federal code section on LexisNexis.

Sign on to Lexis at http://www.lexisnexis.com/lawschool. These seven questions will ask you to locate a federal code section in U.S.C.A. and then answer questions about the code section.

1.   Click on **Research System**. Under **Federal Legal – U.S.**, click on **United States Code Service Titles 1 through 50**. Search U.S.C.S. to find the title and section of the code to answer the following question. Click on Full-Text of Sources Documents and use Terms and Connectors. Which commission prohibits the use of lead-based paint in toys? Answer the question and provide the citation to the code. In *The Bluebook*, use Rule 18.1.2 and T.1.

2.   How current is this section of the code?

3.   Scroll down in this code section to the **Research Guide**. What is the title of the article that appeared in the St. Louis U. L. J. in 1974?

4.   What is the title of the A.L.R. Fed. annotation? **Note:** LexisNexis no longer provides access to full-text A.L.R., however, the citation is still listed.

5.   What is the citation of the C.F.R. (Title and Part) on PHA – owned or leased projects?

6.   Click on the **Shepardize** link at the top. Click on the Shepard's link for 42 USC section 4831(a). Under Citing Decisions for 4831(a), what is the name of the 1983 D.C. Circuit case?

7.   Click your browser's back button. Click on the Shepard's exact match for 42 USC sec. 4831. In addition to cases, does Shepard's provide citations to Secondary Sources for section 4831?

ASSIGNMENT TEN
FEDERAL LEGISLATIVE HISTORY ONLINE
EXERCISE A

GOAL OF THIS ASSIGNMENT:
To acquaint you with the ways to search for legislative history materials on THOMAS, GPO Access, LexisNexis Congressional, and HeinOnline.

In this assignment, you will use two free legislative history websites, THOMAS and GPO Access and two databases that are available by subscription, LexisNexis Congressional (also available on LexisNexis) and HeinOnline. You will have to check with your librarian to see if you have the two subscription databases.

Before you begin working on Questions 1-9, you should spend some time reading the **About THOMAS** link and the **About GPO Access** link.

Questions 1-7 require you to use THOMAS at **http://thomas.loc.gov**. THOMAS is a free U.S. Government web site maintained by the Library of Congress for accessing federal legislative documents, including bill status, bills, resolutions, committee reports, and issues of the *Congressional Record*. THOMAS' strength is the integration of data and documents from many legislative sources, including GPO Access.

We will begin searching the CAN-SPAM Act of 2003, Public Law 108-187. Access **THOMAS**. Click on the **Public Laws** link in the middle column of the THOMAS homepage. This link takes you to a page where you can select Public Laws by Congress. Click on **108** under **Select Congress,** then choose the **108-151 – 108-200 range** and click the **View** button. Scroll down to **187** and click on the **bill number** link.

1. Using the expanded view of the legislative history of this bill, click on the link for **All Information (except text)**. Who is the main sponsor of the bill?

2. On 11/25/2003, the Senate concurred in the House amendment with an amendment by Unanimous Consent in the *Congressional Record*. **Note**: "CR" stands for *Congressional Record*. List the page numbers where this appeared in the *Congressional Record*.

3.   Following from Question 2, click on **page number 15948**. What does Ms. Collins wish her fellow senators?

4.   Click back several times to the **All Information (except text)** for **S. 877**. What is the number of the report issued on 7/16/2003?

5.   If you click on the entry listed under **12/16/2003**, the text of the public law, where does it send you?

You can also search **THOMAS** for bills that are not passed into law. Return to the THOMAS homepage by using the blue **THOMAS** link that appears on the top of every THOMAS page.

6.   Search for a bill that was introduced in 2007, the Safe Climate Act of 2007 (110th Congress). Click on the **Search Multiple, Previous Congress** link in the middle column. Type the name of the act in the **Enter Word/Phrase to Search Bill Text** box. Under **Select Congress**, click on the **110** box and unclick any other box. Now click **Search**. It should locate H.R. 1590. Click on **Bill Summary and Status File**, then Click on **All Information,** then click on **All Actions.** The bill was referred to two committees. Name the two committees.

7.   Did the bill pass into law? **Hint**: Look at the end of the action for this bill.

Next, you will use **GPO Access**, the Government Printing Office's website at **http://www.gpoaccess.gov/legislative.html** to answer Questions 8 and 9. GPO's strength is providing online versions of official documents. GPO offers PDF versions that retain the helpful formatting of the print originals. It is best to read the *Congressional Record* on GPO Access. GPO makes browsing easier. You can retrieve a page in the *Congressional Record* by page number. You can jump to specific words within a large document by using the **Edit/Find** menu option.

8. Under **The Legislative Process**, click on **Public and Private Laws**. Click on **More on GPO's Authentication Initiative.** What does the digital signature, as viewed through the GPO Seal of Authenticity, verify?

9. Next, click on **Public and Private Laws** in the left column. Locate Public Law 108-187 by clicking on **Previous Congresses – Search**. Follow the instructions on how you type a public law number. Once you locate Public Law 108-187, click on **PDF**. You can jump to specific words within a large document by using the Find option. Locate the meaning of "loss" within the law. What section has the meaning of the term "loss"?

Next, you will access **LexisNexis Congressional** for Questions 10-13. This is a subscription database, so check your Law Library's list of databases. If your library subscribes to LexisNexis Congressional database, this same database will be available through your LexisNexis law school subscription. Therefore, you can complete this exercise on either the **LexisNexis Congressional database** or **LexisNexis source Legal > Federal Legal – U.S. > Legislative Histories and Materials > US – CIS Legislative Materials**.

This database is very extensive and nicely arranged. It includes the full text of congressional publications, a bill tracking service and the full text of public laws. Additionally, there is listing of members and committees and political news. If you need help with this database, click on the **How Do I? link** at the top of the home page.

Again, we will search for the legislative history of the CAN-SPAM Act of 2003, Public Law No. 108-187. Using the LexisNexis Congressional database, first, locate **Legislative Histories, Bills & Laws** on the left hand side of the page. Click on it. Click on **Get a Document.** Select **Enter number – Public Law Number.** Enter **108-187** and **Search.**

If you are using LexisNexis to access the Congressional database, **access Legal > Federal Legal – U.S. > Legislative Histories and Materials > US – CIS Legislative Histories**. Type **PL(108-187)** in the search box and click **Search.**

10.   Is the full text of the act available?

11.   Notice that the Legislative History of P.L. 108-187 is very extensive. Scroll through CIS Legislative History Document. Under **Reports**, locate and click on S. Rpt. 108-102. Which Senate committee issued the report?

12.   Return to the Legislative History page. Scroll down the page. Locate the **hearings**. Are the hearings full text?

13.   Return to the **LexisNexis Congressional Home Page. Note**: This page is not available through your school's subscription to LexisNexis. There is a listing for **Hot Topics**, which provides many ideas for writing papers on topics of national importance. Select **Political News/Hot Topics** from the left hand navigation bar. Select **Hot Bills and Hot Topics tab** then click on **Go to Hot Bills & Hot Topics**. State one hot topic listed.

Next, you will search **HeinOnline U.S. Federal Legislative History Library**. Check with your librarian to find out if your library subscribes to this database. It includes selective complete legislative histories on landmark acts. It also includes the finding aid, *Sources of Compiled Legislative Histories* by Nancy P. Johnson. This source includes many law review articles and secondary materials on individual federal laws.

Access **HeinOnline U.S. Federal Legislative History Library,** and then click on **Sources of Compiled Legislative History Database.**

14. Scroll down to and click on the **108ᵗʰ Congress (2003-04)**. Find **Public Law 108-187** and click on **Controlling the Assault of Non-Solicited Pornography and Marketing Act of 2003 or the CAN-Spam Act of 2003**. Which law review included Jason A. Smith's article on spam?

15. On the same page, locate William H. Manz's book on the CAN-SPAM Act. Which documents does it include?

HeinOnline Federal Legislative History database also includes the **U.S. Federal Legislative History Title Collection**. Click on that collection. It is a collection of full-text legislative histories on some of the most important legislation.

16. Click on the **Anticybersquatting Consumer Protection Act**. Under **Cumulative Contents**, click on the **1 (2002)** link. On the left side of the page, scroll down to locate the hearing before the Senate Judiciary Committee. What is the date of this hearing?

ASSIGNMENT TEN
FEDERAL LEGISLATIVE HISTORY ONLINE
EXERCISE B

GOAL OF THIS ASSIGNMENT:

To acquaint you with the ways to search for legislative history materials on Westlaw and LexisNexis.

First, use **Westlaw** at **http://lawschool.westlaw.com**. Refer to Rule 18.1 and its subsections on Commercial Electronic Databases in *The Bluebook*.

Westlaw has extensive legislative history materials. There are several ways to access federal legislative histories; however, if you have a citation to a code section, you should begin your search for legislative history with *United States Code Annotated* on Westlaw.

Begin at **Directory > U.S. Federal Materials > Federal Statutes,** then access the **United States Code Annotated (U.S.C.A.)** database. Assume you are seeking legislative history materials for the "CAN-SPAM" Act. Type in **CAN-SPAM** and you will retrieve several documents. Click on **15 U.S.C.A. § 7707**. Scroll down to **CREDIT(S)**. The CREDITS indicate that the original law passed in 2003 was Public Law No. 108-187. Next, click on **KeyCite – History** located on the left hand side of the screen. KeyCite History lists legislative materials related to the statute. Notice the number of citations to Reports, *Congressional Record*, Testimony, and Presidential Messages. Use this information to answer Questions 1 and 2.

1. Congressional testimony is often difficult to locate on free websites. Fortunately, you can locate it on the commercial databases. Click on the **October 30, 2003 testimony**. Notice it jumps to a reference for S. 877. Which House of Representative Committee sponsored this hearing?

2. When did the President sign the bill into law?

Another way to understand the lawmaking process is to view a graphical illustration of the steps that a bill takes through Congress. This page consolidates the materials needed to research legislative history. To select this graphical illustration, click **Add/Remove Tabs** at the top of any page. Scroll down to **Jurisdictional – Federal** and select **Legislative History – Fed.** Click **Next** at the bottom of the page. Then click **Save**. Next, click on that **tab** and you will view the graphical representation of Congressional Lawmaking Process.

If you click one of the steps, Westlaw displays a page containing a Search page and a list of appropriate databases. Click on **#7 Legislative debate on bill.** **Check Congressional Record.** For Questions 3 and 4, type **"National Women's History Museum Act of 2003"** and click **Search.**

3. On what pages in the Nov. 21, 2003 *Congressional Record* is the act discussed?

4. What is included in the *Congressional Record*?

On Westlaw, the **Legislative History – U.S. Code, 1948 to present (LH)** database includes committee reports as reprinted in the *United States Code Congressional and Administrative News* (USCCAN) from 1948 to the present. To retrieve documents related to a specific act, search the name of the act in the **USCCAN** database for Questions 5 and 6. Click on **Directory > U.S. Federal Materials > Federal Statutes**, then **U.S. Code Congressional & Administrative News** at end of the list, and then **U.S. Code Congressional & Administrative News (USCCAN).**

5. Assume you want to retrieve reports related to the act on **Noxious Plants**. Type in "Noxious Plants" and select **Specific** from the drop down box for Dates. Type **1968** into the box. What is the House Report Number?

6.   Click on the link for the report. Within the committee report, what do the five asterisks represent? **Hint**: Scroll to the end of the report for the Note.

Westlaw offers thousands of federal legislative histories compiled by Government Accountability Office law librarians. The coverage is between 1980 and 1995. The GAO legislative histories are very comprehensive. To access the **GAO legislative histories,** click on **Directory > U.S. Federal Materials > Federal Statutes > US GAO Federal Legislative Histories (FED-LH)** for Questions 7 and 8.

7.   Fill in the template and search for the "Americans with Disabilities Act of 1990." Notice the depth of legislative materials. Click on the Public Law link. Click **Next Part** until you scroll to the end of the list. Who delivered the remarks on the signing of the act?

8.   Lastly, click on **Research Trail**. Notice that Research Trail saves your searches and you can access your work until later in the day and evening. You may download or email your trail. At this point, add a note to your latest entry for later reference. How many research events are in your Research Trail?

Sign off Westlaw.

Next, use **LexisNexis** at **http://www.lexisnexis.com/lawschool**. Refer to Rule 18.1 and its subsections on Commercial Electronic Databases in *The Bluebook*.

In Assignment Ten, Exercise A, you already used the extensive legislative history material on **LexisNexis Congressional**, if your library subscribes to that database. Remember, you can access **LexisNexis Congressional** from either your library's list of databases or from LexisNexis. Additionally, LexisNexis has other ways to search for legislative history materials.

Start in **Research System**. Go to **Search by Source > Federal Legal – U.S. > Legislative Histories and Materials**. Let us return to the National Women's History Museum Act of 2003 and locate committee reports, debates, and news stories for Questions 9–11.

9. Locate Committee Reports, by selecting **Committee Reports** and search for **"National Women's History Museum Act of 2003."** What is the number of the 2003 Senate Report?

10. Return to Legislative Histories and Materials. Click on **Congressional Record and Full–Text Bills**. Search again for the "National Women's History Museum Act of 2003." There are two references to the *Congressional Record* listed. Provide the volume and page for the October 22, 2003 reference.

11. Return to **Search by Source** and click on the **News and Business** tab. You can search for news about new or pending acts in this database. Select **News – Most Recent Two Years**. Search for **"Women's History Museum Act of 2007."** How many articles appear?

Sign off LexisNexis.

ASSIGNMENT ELEVEN
FINDING AND CITING ADMINISTRATIVE MATERIALS
EXERCISE A

GOALS OF THIS ASSIGNMENT:
To acquaint you with finding federal regulations and administrative decisions in your library.
To familiarize you with the rules for citing regulations and administrative decisions in *The Bluebook: A Uniform System of Citation*, 18th ed.

CITATION RULES: You will need to read Rules 14.1-14.3 (including subsections) and refer to tables T.1, T.6, T.10, and T.12. Apply these rules as you determine the correct citation for each regulation and decision. All of the materials in this assignment are U.S. government documents and may be shelved in the government documents area of your library.

The first question requires you to find and cite a regulation in the C.F.R. Cite all federal rules and regulations to the C.F.R. by title, section, and year. Include the name of the regulation if it is commonly known by its name. **Example: 7 C.F.R. § 1902.6 (2008).**

1.   Find and cite the most recent edition of the *Code of Federal Regulations*, section 1214.1106 of Title 14. Do not include the name of the regulation.

The next question requires you to find and cite a regulation in the daily *Federal Register*. Citations of regulations should give the commonly used name (if appropriate), the volume and page on which the regulation begins, and the exact date. When the *Federal Register* indicates where the rule will appear in the C.F.R., give that information in parentheses. **Example: 67 Fed. Reg. 49,599 (July 31, 2002) (to be codified at 38 C.F.R. pt. 20).**

2.   Find the *Federal Register* for March 28, 2008 at p. 16559 and cite the regulation correctly. Do not include the name of the regulation.

Next, you must find a proposed rule (that is, one that is not promulgated) in the *Federal Register* and cite it correctly. When citing proposed rules, follow the form for final rules (see above example), but also add the exact date it was proposed. **Example: 60 Fed. Reg. 3371 (proposed Jan. 17, 1995) (to be codified at 49 C.F.R. pt. 40).**

3. Find the *Federal Register* for April 4, 2008 at p. 18466 and cite it correctly. Do not include the name of the proposed regulation.

Now, find and cite an administrative decision or adjudication. When citing an administrative decision, cite by case name, report, and date - see Rule 14.3. The case name should only be the first-listed private party or subject-matter title. NOTE: If the case does not appear in an official agency reporter, then cite to a looseleaf service; see Rule 19 for details. **Example:** *John Staurulakis, Inc.*, **4 F.C.C.R. 516 (1988).**

4. Find the administrative decision involving Septix Waste, Inc. in volume 346 of the *Decisions and Orders of the National Labor Relations Board.* You may need to seek assistance from your librarian to locate administrative decisions in your library. Provide the full citation of the case.

The *Federal Register*, the C.F.R., and many administrative decisions are online on Westlaw and LexisNexis, which you will use in the following assignment. You can also locate administrative materials on the Internet at http://www.nara.gov and http://www.access.gpo.gov.

GOALS OF THIS ASSIGNMENT:
To acquaint you with finding federal regulations and administrative decisions in your library.
To familiarize you with the rules for citing regulations and administrative decisions in *The Bluebook: A Uniform System of Citation*, 18th ed.

CITATION RULES: You will need to read Rules 14.1-14.3 (including subsections) and refer to tables T.1, T.6, T.10 and T.12. Apply these rules as you determine the correct citation for each regulation and decision. All of the materials in this assignment are U.S. government documents and may be shelved in the government documents area of your library.

The first question requires you to find and cite a regulation in the C.F.R. Cite all federal rules and regulations to the C.F.R. by title, section, and year. Include the name of the regulation if it is commonly known by its name. **Example: 7 C.F.R. § 1902.6 (2008).**

1.   Find and cite the most recent edition of the *Code of Federal Regulations*, section 31.20 of Title 14. Do not include the name of the regulation.

The next question requires you to find and cite a regulation in the daily *Federal Register*. Citations of regulations should give the commonly used name (if appropriate), the volume and page on which the regulation begins, and the exact date. When the *Federal Register* indicates where the rule will appear in the C.F.R., give that information in parentheses. **Example: 67 Fed. Reg. 49,599 (July 31, 2002) (to be codified at 38 C.F.R. pt. 20).**

2.   Find the *Federal Register,* for April 23, 2008 at p. 21807 and cite the regulation correctly. Do not include the name of the regulation.

Next, you must find a proposed rule (that is, one that is not promulgated) in the *Federal Register* and cite it correctly. When citing proposed rules, follow the form for final rules (see above example), but also add the exact date it was proposed. **Example: 60 Fed. Reg. 3371 (proposed Jan. 17, 1995) (to be codified at 49 C.F.R. pt. 40).**

3. Find the *Federal Register* for April 1, 2008 at p.17292 and cite it correctly. Do not include the name of the proposed regulation.

Now, find and cite an administrative decision or adjudication. When citing an administrative decision, cite by case name, report, and date - see Rule 14.3. The case name should only be the first-listed private party or subject-matter title. NOTE: If the case does not appear in an official agency reporter, then cite to a looseleaf service; see Rule 19 for details. **Example: *John Staurulakis, Inc.*, 4 F.C.C.R. 516 (1988).**

4. Find the administrative decision involving Lonnie L. Keeney in volume 22, issue 26 of the Federal Communications Commission Record. You may need to seek assistance from your librarian to locate administrative decisions in your library. Provide the full citation of the case.

The *Federal Register*, the C.F.R., and many administrative decisions are online on Westlaw and LexisNexis, which you will use in the following assignment. You can also locate administrative materials on the Internet at http://www.nara.gov and http://www.access.gpo.gov.

ASSIGNMENT ELEVEN
FINDING AND CITING ADMINISTRATIVE MATERIALS
EXERCISE C

GOALS OF THIS ASSIGNMENT:
To acquaint you with finding federal regulations and administrative decisions on Westlaw.
To familiarize you with the rules for citing regulations and administrative decisions in *The Bluebook: A Uniform System of Citation*, 18th ed.

CITATION RULES: You will need to read Rules 14.1-14.3 (including subsections) and refer to tables T.1, T.6, T.10, and T.12. You also need to refer to Rule 18.1.3 for citing regulations online.

Sign on to Westlaw at http://lawschool.westlaw.com. On Westlaw, Retrieve a Document, then Select Find. The first question requires you to find and cite a regulation in the C.F.R. on Westlaw.

1.   Find and cite the most recent edition of the *Code of Federal Regulations*, section 1214.1106 of Title 14. Do not include the name of the regulation. Refer to Rule 18.1.3.

2.   Using the information for Question 1, how current is the regulation?

The next question requires you to find and cite a regulation in the daily *Federal Register*.

3.   Find the *Federal Register,* vol. 73, for March 28, 2008 at p. 16559 and cite the regulation correctly. Do not include the name of the regulation.

Next, you must find a proposed rule (that is, one that is not promulgated) in the *Federal Register* and cite it correctly.

4.   Find the *Federal Register,* vol. 73, for April 4, 2008 at p. 18466 and cite it correctly. Do not include the name of the proposed regulation. Note: If two regulations are on one printed page, the computer will indicate -01 in the citation. Do not include it in the citation.

Now, find and cite an administrative decision or adjudication. When citing an administrative decision, cite by case name, report, and date - see Rule 14.3. The case name should only be the first-listed private party or subject-matter title.

5.   Find the administrative decision involving Lonnie L. Keeney in volume 22 of the *Federal Communications Commission Record.* Go to the main **Directory**. Click on the following sequence: **U.S. Federal Materials > Federal Administrative Decisions > Federal Communications – FCC Record.** Conduct a **Title** field search for the decision.

6.   Find the administrative decision involving Septix Waste, Inc. in volume 346, No. 50 of the *Decisions and Orders of the National Labor Relations Board.* Note: Westlaw cites to decision numbers rather than page numbers. Look at the parallel cites to optain the page number from the print volume. Go to the main **Directory**. Click on the following sequence: **U.S. Federal Materials > Federal Administrative Decisions > National Labor Relations Board – Board and ALJ Decisions Combined.** Conduct a **Title** field search for the decision.

FINDING AND CITING ADMINISTRATIVE MATERIALS
EXERCISE D

GOALS OF THIS ASSIGNMENT:
To acquaint you with finding federal regulations and administrative decisions on LexisNexis.
To familiarize you with the rules for citing regulations and administrative decisions in _The Bluebook: A Uniform System of Citation_, 18th ed.

CITATION RULES: You will need to read Rules 14.1-14.3 (including subsections) and refer to tables T.1, T.6, T.10, and T.12. You also need to refer to Rule 18.1.3 for citing regulations online.

> **Sign on to Lexis at http://www.lexisnexis.com/lawschool and use Get a Document. The first question requires you to find and cite a regulation in the C.F.R. on LexisNexis.**

1. Get and cite the most recent edition of the _Code of Federal Regulations_, section 1214.1106 of Title 14. Do not include the name of the regulation. Refer to Rule 18.1.3.

2. Using the information for Question 1, how current is the regulation?

> **The next question requires you to find and cite a regulation in the daily _Federal Register_.**

3. Get the _Federal Register,_ vol. 73, for March 28, 2008 at p. 16559 and cite the regulation correctly. Do not include the name of the regulation.

> **Next, you must find a proposed rule (that is, one that is not promulgated) in the _Federal Register_ and cite it correctly.**

4.   Get the *Federal Register,* vol. 73, for April 4, 2008 at p. 18466 and cite it correctly. Do not include the name of the proposed regulation. Do not include it in the citation.

Now, find and cite an administrative decision or adjudication. When citing an administrative decision, cite by case name, report, and date - see Rule 14.3. The case name should only be the first-listed private party or subject-matter title.

5.   Get the administrative decision involving Lonnie L. Keeney in volume 22 of the *Federal Communications Commission Record*. Go to **Research System > Federal Legal – U.S. > Administrative Agency Materials > Individual Agencies > Federal Communications Commission Decisions**. Conduct a **Name** segment search for your decision.

6.   Get the administrative decision involving Septix Waste, Inc. in volume 346 of the *Decisions and Orders of the National Labor Relations Board*. Go to **Research System > Federal Legal – U.S. > Administrative Agency Materials > Individual Agencies > National Labor Relations Board Decisions & General Counsel Memos**. Conduct a **Name** segment search for your decision.

ASSIGNMENT TWELVE
FEDERAL ADMINISTRATIVE RULES AND REGULATIONS
EXERCISE A

GOALS OF THIS ASSIGNMENT:
To develop your ability to find printed federal final regulations on a specific topic or issued pursuant to authority granted by a particular statute.
To update a regulation.
To search the C.F.R. and *LSA: List of Sections Affected* on the Internet.

To answer Questions 1-2, use the Index volume to the *Code of Federal Regulations* (most current year), published by the Government Printing Office. Use the print volumes to answer Questions 1-6.

1. Using the Parallel Table of Authorities and Rules, labeled "authorities," in the Index volume, state which title and part of the C.F.R. were adopted under the authority of **32 U.S.C. § 110**. By using this table you can find regulations if you already have the U.S.C. citation.

2. Now, use the subject index in the same Index volume. Find and cite the regulations on nutritional quality guidelines for foods.

    Reshelve the Index volume.

3. Find the text of the regulation part from the previous question. What is the statutory authority for the regulation part? State the **first** reference to the U.S.C. as printed in the C.F.R.

4. Where did the first regulation from the part in Question 2 appear in the *Federal Register*? State the source note as printed in the C.F.R.

To update the C.F.R. use the slim pamphlet, *LSA: List of CFR Sections Affected*. Use the *LSA: List of CFR Sections Affected* to answer Questions 5 and 6.

5. Using the *LSA: List of CFR Sections Affected*, March 2007, determine if any change occurred in 21 C.F.R. § 71.1(c). What is the status of that section?

6. Where would you find this change in the 2007 *Federal Register*?

Use the Internet to answer Questions 7 and 8.

7. Repeat Question 2 using the e-CFR website at http://ecfr.gpoaccess.gov. This website is an editorial compilation of C.F.R. material and *Federal Register* amendments. It is updated daily. What search terms led you to the regulation? **Hint**: When performing search, use the **Boolean** search link under Advanced Search on the left. You may have to scroll down the page to find the regulation.

8. Go to the GPO website at http://www.gpoaccess.gov.lsa/browse.html and repeat Question 5. Click on the *LSA: List of CFR Sections Affected* for **March 2007**. Scroll down to your title and click the link on the right. Did you find the same answer to Question 5?

GOALS OF THIS ASSIGNMENT:
To develop your ability to find printed federal final regulations on a specific topic or issued pursuant to authority granted by a particular statute.
To update a regulation.
To search the C.F.R. and *LSA: List of Sections Affected* on the Internet.

To answer Questions 1-2, use the Index volume to the *Code of Federal Regulations* (most current year), published by the Government Printing Office. Use the print volumes to answer Questions 1-6.

1. Using the Parallel Table of Authorities and Rules, labeled "authorities," in the Index volume, state which title and part of the C.F.R. were adopted under the authority of **39 U.S.C. § 406.** By using this table you can find regulations if you already have the U.S.C. citation.

2. Now, use the subject index in the same Index volume. Find and cite the regulations on security control of air traffic.

   Reshelve the Index volume.

3. Find the text of the regulation part from the previous question. What is the statutory authority for the regulation part? State the **first** reference to the U.S.C. as printed in the C.F.R.

4. Where did the first regulation from the part in Question 2 appear in the *Federal Register*? State the source note as printed in the C.F.R.

To update the C.F.R. use the slim pamphlet, *LSA: List of CFR Sections Affected*. Use the *LSA: List of CFR. Sections Affected* to answer Questions 5 and 6.

5. Using the *LSA: List of CFR Sections Affected*, February 2008, determine if any change occurred in 48 C.F.R. § 202.101. What is the status of that section?

6. Where would you find this change in the 2007 *Federal Register*?

Use the Internet to answer Questions 7 and 8.

7. Repeat Question 2 using the e-CFR website at http://ecfr.gpoaccess.gov. This website is an editorial compilation of C.F.R. material and *Federal Register* amendments. It is updated daily. What search terms led you to the regulation? **Hint**: When performing search, use the **Boolean** search link under Advanced Search on the left. Type in your C.F.R. title number in the **Enter a Title Number** box. Also, search for your keywords with **Part**.

8. Go to the GPO website at http://www.gpoaccess.gov/lsa/browse.html and repeat Question 5. Click on the *LSA: List of CFR Sections Affected* for **February 2008**. Scroll down to your title and click the link on the right. Did you find the same answer to Question 5?

GOALS OF THIS ASSIGNMENT:
To locate codified regulations on Westlaw.

Sign on to Westlaw at http://lawschool.westlaw.com. Begin with Directory, then click on U.S. Federal Materials > Administrative Rules & Regulations > Code of Federal Regulations – Current Version to answer Questions 1-7.

1. Find the regulation on nutritional quality guidelines in food and provide the citation to the C.F.R. Scroll down to the section on **General principles**. In *The Bluebook*, use Rule 18.1.3 but omit the name of the regulation.

2. Examine the text of the regulation under § 104.5. What is the authority of the regulation?

3. How current is this regulation?

4. On Westlaw, is it necessary to update a C.F.R. citation using the *Federal Register*?

5. Next, click on **KeyCite – Citing References**. What is the title of the 1996 law review article?

6.   In addition to other materials, does KeyCite provide citations to the *Federal Register*?

7.   Next click on the **Prior Versions** under **RegulationsPlus, Historical** on the left. In research, what would be the value of an earlier edition of the C.F.R.?

ASSIGNMENT TWELVE
FEDERAL ADMINISTRATIVE RULES AND REGULATIONS
EXERCISE D

GOALS OF THIS ASSIGNMENT:
To locate codified regulations on LexisNexis.

Sign on to LexisNexis at http://www.lexisnexis.com/lawschool. Click on Legal > Federal Legal – U.S. > CFR - Code of Federal Regulations to answer Questions 1-7.

1. Find the regulation on nutritional quality guidelines in food and provide the citation to the C.F.R. Scroll down to the section on **General principles**. In *The Bluebook*, use Rule 18.1.3 but omit the name of the regulation.

2. Examine the text of the regulation under § 104.5. On what page did this regulation appear in the 1977 *Federal Register*?

3. How current is this regulation?

4. On LexisNexis, is it necessary to update a C.F.R. citation suing the *Federal Register*?

5. In your examination of the regulation, what is the authority of the regulation?

6.   Can you **Shepardize** this regulation from this location in LexisNexis?

7.   Is it possible to Shepardize some regulations?   How did you determine this
        answer?

ASSIGNMENT THIRTEEN
REVIEW—FINDING STATUTES AND REGULATIONS
EXERCISE A

GOAL OF THIS ASSIGNMENT:
Require you to use statutes and regulations to solve research problems.

In this assignment, you will review statutory and regulatory research. You will find statutory law, legislative history, and regulations.

You are clerking for a lawyer during the summer. Your supervising lawyer has an elderly client who continues to receive abusive **telemarketing** calls, even though he is on the **"do-not-call"** registry. The lawyer asks you to research the **telemarketing rules** under the act. You begin your research with the federal annotated code since the question involves a federal law.

1. Use the Index in U.S.C.A. to determine the appropriate code section. Look up the act and answer Questions 1-6.

   a. What is the correct citation to the code section that deals with the telemarketing rules? **Note**: Use Rule 12 and table T.1 in *The Bluebook*. **Hint**: Make sure you check the pocket part.

   b. Does the act address abusive telemarketing acts?

2. Examine the section. What is the Public Law number of the 1994 act?

3. Under **Library References**, what is the section number to *West's Federal Practice Manual* for telephone consumer protection?

4.   Under **Historical and Statutory Notes,** find references to the legislative history of the 1994 act. Obtain the citation to U.S.C.C.A.N. On what page of the 1994 U.S.C.C.A.N. does the legislative history begin?

5.   Where would you find regulations on telemarketing sales rules in the C.F.R.? **Hint**: Look at the **Library References** at the beginning of Chapter 87.

6.   Next, examine the **Notes of Decisions**. Find a 2006 district court case on automatic dialers. What is the name of the case?

Reshelve U.S.C.A. and find U.S.C.C.A.N.

7.   Examine the legislative history in the 1994 U.S.C.C.A.N. from Question 4. Which House report is reprinted in U.S.C.C.A.N.? **Hint**: Look in the Legislative History pages of the 1994 U.S.C.C.A.N.

Reshelve U.S.C.C.A.N. and find the C.F.R.

8.   Look up the regulation from Question 5 in the C.F.R. What is the definition of "upselling?"

GOAL OF THIS ASSIGNMENT:
Require you to use statutes and regulations to solve research problems.

In this assignment, you will review statutory and regulatory research. You will find statutory law, legislative history, and regulations.

You are clerking for a lawyer during the summer. Your supervising lawyer has a client who wants to file a complaint with the Secretary of Transportation concerning an **aircraft** incident that the client hopes will be the subject of an **investigation**. You begin your research with the federal annotated code since the question involves a federal law.

1.   Use the Index in U.S.C.A. to determine the appropriate code section. Look up the act and answer Questions 1-6.

      a.   What is the correct citation to the code section concerning complaints and investigations? **Note**: Use Rule 12 and table T.1 in *The Bluebook*.

      b.   Must the complaint be in writing?

2.   Examine the section. What is the Public Law number of the 2001 amendment?

3.   Under **Library References**, what is the West topic and key number on the topic?

4.   Under **Historical and Statutory Notes**, find references to the legislative history of the 2001 act. Obtain the citation to U.S.C.C.A.N. On what page of the 2001 U.S.C.C.A.N. does the legislative history begin?

5.   Where would you find regulations on rules of practice for informal investigations in the C.F.R.?

6.   Next, examine the **Notes of Decisions**. Find a 1976 Court of Appeals case on notice and opportunity for hearing. What is the name of the case?

Reshelve U.S.C.A. and find U.S.C.C.A.N.

7.   Examine the legislative history in the 2001 U.S.C.C.A.N. from Question 4. Which House conference report is reprinted in U.S.C.C.A.N.? **Hint**: Look in the Legislative History pages of the 2001 U.S.C.C.A.N.

Reshelve U.S.C.C.A.N. and find the C.F.R.

8.   Look up the regulation from Question 5 in the C.F.R. How are investigations initiated?

ASSIGNMENT THIRTEEN
REVIEW—FINDING STATUTES AND REGULATIONS
EXERCISE C

GOAL OF THIS ASSIGNMENT:
Require you to use statutes and regulations to solve research problems on Westlaw

In this assignment, you will review statutory and regulatory research using Westlaw.

You are clerking for a lawyer during the summer. Your supervising lawyer has an elderly client who continues to receive abusive telemarketing calls, even though he is on the "do-not-call" registry. The lawyer asks you to research the **telemarketing rules** under the act. You begin your research with the federal annotated code since the question involves a federal law.

Sign on to Westlaw at http://lawschool.westlaw.com.

1. Go to the U.S.C.A. database: **Directory > U.S. Federal materials > Federal Statutes > United States Code Annotated (U.S.C.A.).** Conduct a search to find the appropriate code section that deals with telemarketing rules under the Telemarketing and Consumer Fraud and Abuse Prevention Act. Click on the section and answer Questions 1–8.

    a. What is the correct citation to the code section? **Note:** Use Rule 18.1.2 and table T.1 in *The Bluebook*.

    b. Does the act address abusive telemarketing acts?

2. How current is this section of the code?

3. Examine the section. What is the Public Law number of the 1994 act?

4. Under **Library References**, what is the reference to *Corpus Juris Secundum* for home solicitation contracts?

5.   Next, examine the Notes of Decisions. Find a 2006 district court case on automatic dialers. What is the name of the case?

6.   Click **Citing References** under **KeyCite Proposed Legislation**. Scroll down to **Registers (U.S.A.).** What is the date of the most recent proposed regulation on telemarketing sales rules?

7.   Click on **History** under **KeyCite Proposed Legislation**. Locate House Report for Pub. L. No. 103-297. What is the report number?

8.   Scroll to the top of the page for **History**. What is the date of the Proposed Legislation?

ASSIGNMENT THIRTEEN
REVIEW—FINDING STATUTES AND REGULATIONS
EXERCISE D

GOAL OF THIS ASSIGNMENT:
Require you to use statutes and regulations to solve research problems using LexisNexis.

Sign on to LexisNexis at http://www.lexisnexis.com/lawschool.

In this assignment, you will review statutory and regulatory research.

You are clerking for a lawyer during the summer. Your supervising lawyer has a client who wants to file a complaint with the **Secretary of Transportation** concerning an **aviation** incident that the client hopes will be the subject of an **investigation**. The lawyer wants you to research if the **complaint** must be in **writing**. You begin your research with the federal annotated code since the question involves a federal law.

1.   Select the U.S.C.S. source: **Legal > Federal Legal – U.S. > United States Code Service (USCS) Materials > United States Code Service – Titles 1 through 50.** Conduct a search to find the appropriate code section for putting a complaint in writing to the Secretary of Transportation to get an investigation of an aviation incident. Look up the act and answer Questions 1-8.

      a.   What is the correct citation to the code section? **Note:** Use Rule 18.1.2 and table T.1 in *The Bluebook.*

      b.   In code section (a), the Secretary must find what in order to conduct an investigation?

2.   How current is this section of the code?

3.   Examine the section. What is the Public Law number of the 2001 amendment?

4.   Under **Research Guide**, what is the Am. Jur. 2d citation on Aviation?

5.   Under **Code of Federal Regulations**, where would you find regulations on tariffs?

6.   Scroll down to the **Interpretive Notes and Decisions**. Find a 1981 Court of Appeals case on notice and opportunity for hearing. What is the name of the case?

7.   Click on **Shepardize**. Click on exact match. Locate the Second Circuit Court of Appeals case that interpreted the case. What is the name of the case?

8.   Scroll up to the Legislative History section of your Shepard's display. What is the cite to the Statute at Large that amended this code section?

ASSIGNMENT FOURTEEN
SECONDARY AUTHORITY
EXERCISE A

GOALS OF THIS ASSIGNMENT:
To familiarize you with one of two major legal encyclopedias and your state legal encyclopedia.
To introduce you to the legal periodical indexes and how to cite legal periodical articles – in either print or online.
To show you how to find treatises in your library.
To introduce you to looseleaf services – either in print or online.

Answer Questions 1-2 using _American Jurisprudence 2d._

1.   Begin in the Index volumes. Provide the complete citation of the section that defines **escheat**. Use _Bluebook_ form, Rule 15.8(a).

2.   Look up the section. This section indicates that the term traditionally covers the reversion of real property to the state. However, the term is also used where a government acquires title to abandoned personal property. State the name of the Louisiana case that is cited for this proposition.

3.   Does your state have a legal encyclopedia? If so, state the title of the encyclopedia.

To answer Questions 4 and 5, use either _LegalTrac_ or _Index to Legal Periodicals and Books_ in print. Refer to Rule 16 and table T.13. Look at the actual articles to cite them.

4.   Provide the complete citation to a 2004 article proposing a change to the assault and battery exception under federal tort law. Online, use the basic search.

5.   State the citation of the March 2008 article authored by Mark Hansen that appeared in the *ABA Journal* on DNA. **Note**: This journal is not consecutively paged, so follow Rule 16.4.

6.   If your law library holds this issue, where is this periodical in your library? Provide either a row number or call number.

You should use your library's online catalog to answer questions 7 and 8.

7.   Find the 2004 hornbook on constitutional law by John E. Nowak and Ronald D. Rotunda in your library. Cite it according to Rule 15.

8.   Find the 2006 nutshell on contracts by Anthony M. Skrocki and Claude D. Rohwer. Provide the call number or location of the book in your library.

Answer questions 9 and 10 using *ABA/BNA Lawyers' Manual On Professional Conduct* in print or online. Hint for online searchers: Browse the website for the Ethics Opinions area, use the ABA Ethics Opinions link, and type your search into the search box at the top of the page.

9. State the citation to the 2006 ABA Formal Ethics Opinion on the review and use of metadata in email. Cite it according to Rule 12.8.6.

10. Browse the text of the ethics opinion from question 9. What Model Rules does the opinion state is the most closely applicable rule to the metadata issue? Cite the answer according to Rules 12.8.5 and 12.8.6.

GOALS OF THIS ASSIGNMENT:
To familiarize you with the two major legal encyclopedias and your state legal encyclopedia.
To introduce you to the legal periodical indexes and how to cite legal periodical articles, in either print or online.
To show you how to find treatises in your library.
To introduce you to looseleaf services, either in print or online.

Answer Questions 1-2 using *American Jurisprudence 2d.*

1. Begin in the Index volumes. Provide the complete citation to the section that discusses using obscenity on a phone. Use *Bluebook* form, Rule 15.8(a).

2. Look up the section. This section indicates anyone who makes an obscene call may be fined or imprisoned or both. Which act governs?

3. Does your state have a legal encyclopedia? If so, state the title of the encyclopedia.

To answer Questions 4 and 5, use either *LegalTrac* or *Index to Legal Periodicals and Books* in print. Refer to Rule 16 and table T.13. Look at the actual articles to cite them.

4.   Provide the complete citation to a 2004 article on Buddhist legal studies. Online, use the basic search.

5.   State the citation of the January 2008 article authored by Dennis Kennedy that appeared in the ABA Journal. **Note**: This journal is not consecutively paged, so follow Rule 16.4.

6.   If your law library holds the issue from Question 5, where is this periodical in your library? Provide either a row number or call number.

You should use your library's online catalog to answer questions 7 and 8.

7.   Find the 2003 hornbook on criminal law by Wayne R. Lafave in your library. Cite it according to Rule 15.

8.   Find the 2005 nutshell on torts by Edward J. Kionka. Provide the call number or location of the book in your library.

Answer questions **9** and **10** using *CCH Standard Federal Tax Reporter* in print or online. Hint for online searchers using the CCH Tax Research Network: Choose the tab for Federal Tax, then *Standard Federal Income Tax Reporter*, and then *Standard Federal Income Tax Reporter* - Select All. Type query in search box.

9.   State the paragraph number that examines business expenses of a law student.

10.   Browse the text of the answer from Question 9. What is the name of the case that states that the law student's losses arising from his part-time legal research were not deductible?

ASSIGNMENT FOURTEEN
SECONDARY AUTHORITY
EXERCISE C

GOALS OF THIS ASSIGNMENT:
To familiarize you with *American Jurisprudence 2d* on Westlaw.
To teach you how to find periodical articles on Westlaw.
To introduce you to a looseleaf service online.

Sign on to Westlaw at http:/lawschool.westlaw.com.

Answer questions 1-2 using the *American Jurisprudence 2d* database. Click on Directory > Treatises, CLEs, Practice Guides > American Jurisprudence 2d.

1. Search for the entry that discusses using obscenity on a phone. What is the Am. Jur. 2d topic and section number?

2. Read the section. The section indicates a person who violates this law may be fined, imprisoned, or both. What is the citation to the U.S.C.A. that provides this information?

To answer Questions 3-5, use the Legal Resource Index (LRI) database. This database is based on the print publication *Current Law Index*. Refer to Rules 16, 18.1.4, and table T.13.

3. Click on **Directory > Legal Periodical > Periodical Indexes > Legal Resource Index (LRI).** Provide the citation to the 2007 article on frivolous litigation.

4. Is the full text of the article available?

5. Click to go to the article. Look at the **Citing References** under KeyCite. What type of materials do you find?

 Answer question 6 using *ABA/BNA Lawyers' Manual on Professional Conduct* on Westlaw. If your library does not subscribe to BNA looseleaf services in an online format, the services will not be on Westlaw. Check with your librarian. Under Directory, search the Westlaw Directory for BNA. Once you locate the lists of BNA services, scroll to ABA/BNA Lawyers' Manual on Professional Conduct.

6. Locate 2006 reports on the use of metadata by lawyers. How many documents are in your results?

ASSIGNMENT FOURTEEN
SECONDARY AUTHORITY
EXERCISE D

GOALS OF THIS ASSIGNMENT:
To familiarize you with *American Jurisprudence 2d* on LexisNexis.
To teach you how to find periodical articles on LexisNexis.
To introduce you to a looseleaf service online.

Sign on to LexisNexis http://www.lexisnexis.com/lawschool.

Answer questions 1-2 using the *American Jurisprudence 2d* source. Go to Legal > Secondary Legal > Jurisprudence and Encyclopedias > American Jurisprudence 2d.

1.   Search for the entry that discusses that a person may be fined for using obscene language on a phone. What is the Am. Jur. 2d topic and section number?

2.   Read the section. The section indicates a person who violates this law may be fined, imprisoned, or both. What is the citation to the U.S.C.A. that provides this information?

To answer Questions 3-5, use the Legal Resource Index source. This source is based on the print publication *Current Law Index*. Refer to Rules 16, 18.1.4, and table T.13. Go to Legal > Secondary Legal > Annotations & Indexes > Legal Resource Index.

3.   Provide the citation to the 2004 article on the origins of the law school admissions test.

4.   Is there a link from the Index to the full text of the article?

Retrieve the article from Question 3 using Get a Document.

5.   Is it possible to shepardize this article?

Answer question 6 using *ABA/BNA Lawyers' Manual on Professional Conduct* on LexisNexis. If your library does not subscribe to BNA looseleaf services in an online format, the services will not be on LexisNexis. Check with your librarian. Go to Legal > Secondary Legal > BNA > ABA/BNA Lawyers' Manual on Professional Conduct.

6.   Conduct a search for the 2006 ABA Formal Ethics Opinion on the review and use of metadata. On what date was the opinion issued?

ASSIGNMENT FIFTEEN
REVIEW—FINDING SECONDARY AUTHORITY
EXERCISE A

GOALS OF THIS ASSIGNMENT:
To review the use of sources of secondary authority.
To emphasize how the various publications cross-reference users to other materials.

You are a clerk in a large general practice law firm in California. One day, Mary and Sue make an appointment to talk to Eileen, an attorney in your firm. Mary and Sue have dissolved their partnership; however, they have one child. There is now a dispute over the partners' rights to visitation with the child.

Since Eileen has never dealt with this aspect of family law, she asks you to find out some general information to counsel her client when she visits her office. Eileen wants to read some background information before she delves into cases.

1. Into what broad areas of the law does this question fall?

2. Using your online catalog, find a treatise in your library on visitation rights and custody. List the author, title, and date of publication.

3. Use one of the periodical indexes, such as LegalTrac online or *Index to Periodicals and Books* in print. Check your list of databases in your law library. Find a 2005 article that discusses visitation rights within the dissolution of a same-sex marriage. The article appeared in the **Georgetown Journal of Gender and the Law**. Find the article in your library and cite it according to Rule 16 and table T.13 of *The Bluebook*.

4.   Another good source of secondary authority is A.L.R. Use the A.L.R. Index and find an A.L.R.5th annotation published in 2000 on Mary and Sue's issue of same sex partners and child custody. Look up the annotation and provide the citation according to Rule 16.6.6.

5.   Now examine the beginning of the A.L.R. annotation. Note the different types of cross references to other publications and related annotations. What is the section number to Am. Jur. 2d under the topic *Divorce and Separation*, where you would find a discussion related to this topic?

6.   *American Jurisprudence 2d* may also provide background information on an area of unfamiliar law. Find the topic and section of Am. Jur. 2d in your library from Question 5 and answer the following question. Does a nonparent in a same sex relationship have a right to custody or visitation with a child born to the other party when the relationship is terminated?

GOALS OF THIS ASSIGNMENT:
To review the use of sources of secondary authority.
To emphasize how the various publications cross-reference users to other materials.

Jason is a clerk in a large firm. One of the partners hands Jason an assignment and Jason is puzzled by how to begin his research. The assignment questions whether the copying of a trademark in parody constitutes infringement in violation of federal law.

Since Jason has never dealt with this aspect of trademark, he wants to read some background information before he delves into cases.

1. Into what broad areas of the law does this question fall?

2. Using your online catalog, find a treatise in your library on trademark protection. List the author, title, and date of publication.

3. Use one of the periodical indexes, such as LegalTrac online or *Index to Periodicals and Books* in print. Check your list of databases in your law library. Find a 2004 article that discusses trademark parody. The article appeared in the **Santa Clara Law Review**. Find the article in your library and cite it according to Rule 16 and table T.13 of *The Bluebook*. **Note:** You should find the article in the journal to cite it correctly.

4.   Another good source of secondary authority is A.L.R. Use the A.L.R. Index and find an A.L.R. Fed. annotation published in 2002 on the issue of parody and trademark. Look up the annotation and provide the citation according to Rule 16.6.6. **NOTE**: Remember to check the pocket part.

5.   Now examine the beginning of the A.L.R. annotation. Note the different types of research references to other publications and related annotations. What are the **first three sections** listed in Am. Jur. 2d where you would find a discussion under the topic *Trademarks and Tradenames*?

6.   *American Jurisprudence 2d* may also provide background information on an area of unfamiliar law. Find volume 74 of Am. Jur. 2d. Look section 118 of the topic *Trademarks and Tradenames* in your library and answer the following question. What is the name of the federal act controls cybersquatting?

GOALS OF THIS ASSIGNMENT:
To review the use of sources of secondary authority using Westlaw.
To emphasize how the various publications cross-reference users to other materials.

You are a clerk in a large general practice law firm in California. One day, Mary and Sue make an appointment to talk to Eileen, an attorney in your firm. Mary and Sue have dissolved their partnership; however, they have one child. There is now a dispute over the partners' rights to visitation with the child.

Since Eileen has never dealt with this aspect of family law, she asks you to find out some general information to counsel her client when she visits her office. Eileen wants to read some background information before she delves into cases.

Sign on to Westlaw at http://lawschool.westlaw.com.

Using Westlaw, begin with the Directory > Treatises, CLEs, Practice Guides > California Family Law Report – California Family Law Practice to answer Questions 1-3.

1. Search for a **California Family Law Report** on adoptions by domestic partners. What is the section number for the stepparent adoptions by domestic partners?

2. Using the answer for Question 1, **click** on the citation to the California code. What is the section number to the Family Code?

3. Next, **KeyCite** the California code citation by **clicking** on **Citing References**. Scroll down to **Secondary Sources**. Who is the author of the treatise, *Summary of California Law (California Summary)*?

Next, use the Directory > Legal Periodicals & Current Awareness > Periodical Indexes > Legal Resource Index to answer Question 4.

4.   Locate an article 1996 article on same-sex visitation and adoption cases by Catherine Connolly. The article appeared in **Behavioral Science and the Law**. Cite the article according to Rule 16 of *The Bluebook.*

Next, use the Directory > Treatises, CLEs, Practice Guides > Westlaw eforms: State Courts and Agencies to answer Question 5.

5.   Locate California forms on stepparent adoption. On the search page, select **California** under Limit by State. What agency is responsible for the forms?

Lastly, go to Directory > Legal Periodicals & Current Awareness > Legal Newspaper Databases > American Lawyer to answer Question 6.

6.   Find a June 2004 article in **American Lawyer** on same-sex marriage litigation. Where did the litigation take place in the article?

ASSIGNMENT FIFTEEN
REVIEW—FINDING SECONDARY AUTHORITY
EXERCISE D

GOALS OF THIS ASSIGNMENT:
To review the use of sources of secondary authority using LexisNexis.
To emphasize how the various publications cross-reference users to other materials.

Jason is a clerk in a large law firm. One of the partners hands Jason an assignment and Jason is puzzled by how to begin his research. The assignment questions whether the copying of a trademark in parody constitutes infringement in violation of federal law.

Since Jason has never dealt with this aspect of trademark, he wants to read some background information before he delves into cases.

Sign on to LexisNexis at http://www.lexisnexis.com/lawschool.

Using LexisNexis, begin with Legal > Secondary Legal > Matthew Bender® > By Area of Law > Trademarks, Unfair Competition & Trade Secrets > Trademark and Unfair Competition Deskbook to answer Questions 1-3.

1. Search for parody and satire in the Deskbook. How many citations are listed?

2. Click on the link for Chapter 8, Special Defenses and Limitations § 8.06 Permitted Use. Scroll down to **[6] Parody and Satire**. Click on the *Cliff Notes* case. What is the citation to the case in F.2d?

3. Next, Shepardize the case. Are there citations to court documents? **Hint:** You may want to click on the **FOCUS-Restrict By** link and scroll down to **Other**.

Next, click the Search tab > Legal > Secondary Legal > Law Reviews & Journals > Legal Resource Index to answer Question 4

4.   Locate an article 2006 article on trademark and parody. The article appeared in the **Washington University Law Review**. Cite the article according to Rule 16 of *The Bluebook*.

Next, click the Search tab > Legal > Secondary Legal > Forms & Agreements > By Area of Law > Intellectual Property > Federal Intellectual Property Litigation LexisNexis Forms to answer Question 5.

5.   Locate a form on nonobviousness of the Raun invention. What is the number of the form for the appellant's principal brief?

Lastly, click the Search tab > Legal News > Legal News by Practice Area > Trademarks > MH Legal Articles – Trademarks Law to answer Question 6.

6.   Search for the article on **Barney the Dinosaur**. What is the date of the article?